HOW TO
ADD A ROOM
TO YOUR HOUSE

HOW TO
ADD A ROOM
TO YOUR HOUSE

A Step-By-Step Guide
to Building It Yourself

TOM PHILBIN and
FRITZ KOELBEL

Charles Scribner's Sons
New York

Construction drawings are by Barbara Koelbel.
Drawings of room additions are by Joseph Dolce.

Copyright © 1980 Thomas Philbin and Fritz Koelbel

Library of Congress Cataloging in Publication Data

Philbin, Thomas, 1934–
    How to add a room to your house.

    1. Dwellings—Remodeling—Amateurs' manuals.
2. Building—Amateurs' manuals. I. Koelbel,
Fritz, 1930–   joint author. II. Title.
TH4816.P49   643'.7   80-16054
ISBN 0-684-16494-9

1 3 5 7 9 11 13 15 17 19 V/C 20 18 16 14 12 10 8 6 4 2

Printed in the United States of America

CONTENTS

INTRODUCTION

Getting the Most from This Book

The structure of this book follows the progress of a typical room addition. It starts with the foundation and ends with the application of Sheetrock to walls and ceilings—that is, up to the point where finish materials are installed inside.

To derive maximum benefit from this book, it is suggested that you first read it through—leisurely—from cover to cover. At first glance the building of a room addition may seem like an impossible task. In fact, it isn't. If you have a working knowledge of tools and perhaps have built a birdhouse or two, the job needn't be that complicated or intimidating. Indeed, even if you have never built anything, you can achieve good results. As you read this book, you will notice that techniques tend to be repeated. What at first seems mystifying becomes commonplace.

There are quite a few details involved in adding a room or rooms to your home, details that will become evident by careful reading. For example, you will learn about the advantages and disadvantages of various types of construction, and based on your home and its particular topography, you will be able to decide which is best.

Though there are only four basic types of roofs (gable, hip, shed, and flat), three types of foundations (crawl space, full foundation, and slab), a floor that is level or not level with the existing floor, and the option to make the addition one or more stories high, combining these elements will give you a tremendous range of choices. Mathematically, it works out to forty-eight. For example, you may decide that a one-story, gable-roof addition is best, that the floor must be level with your home, and that it must have a full foundation. Fine. But by varying it a bit —putting in a hip roof instead, or a slab foundation, or flat roof and a slab foundation, the acceptable possibilities add up quickly (Figs. 1–12).

In deciding what kind of addition to build, examine magazines, other books, and, most important, homes in your neighborhood that have been extended. From this book, you will learn about the feasibility and, to some degree, the appearance of any new construction. But you may find something that will look perfect on your home from one of these other sources. The important thing to remember is to make an addition look like a natural part of your home, not something "tacked on" (Figs. 13–15).

This book will enable you to build any of the forty-eight variations of additions mentioned above. There is information on all types of roofs, on the various foundations, and on joining the addition to existing construc-tions, as well as on how to build an addition with *more than one* story.

Special note: USE GOOD TOOLS.

When extending your home, it is important to use good tools. If you don't have a good hammer, circular saw, drill, level, and the like in your tool kit, good ones will be well worth the investment.

There are actually two keys to doing a good job when adding a room. One is to proceed methodically and carefully, not going from one thing to the next until you understand completely what is required. Trying to rush the procedure is almost sure to lead to problems. The other key is to use your measuring tools frequently. Every measurement you take should be done twice. And keep your level in constant use. When using the level, incidentally, make sure that its surface is clean. Even a little grit can throw it off, and on a very long span this can be translated into a significant error. Another factor to remember is that various brands of measuring tape give different measurements—ensure that everyone involved in the construction uses the same brand of tape.

T.P.
F.K.
May 1980

Figure 1. This addition has a gable roof and is set on a slab foundation—elements that blend nicely with the existing house.

Figure 2. In this addition, a shed roof intersects a sloping roof. Windows in the foundation indicate that it is a full foundation. Note also that the floor of addition is in line with the floor of the existing home.

Figure 3. A flat roof and full foundation is another combination. The flat roof serves as a deck with access from the second-floor rooms.

Figure 4. Shed roof of this addition abuts a straight wall. Foundation is a crawl-space type, and in this case the floor of the addition would be lower than the existing floor.

Figure 5. Another example of a flat roof, which could also have been a gable type to match the house. The foundation is a slab.

Figure 6. The hip-roofed addition blends nicely into the house, with its existing hip roof. The crawl-space foundation has been constructed so that the floor of the addition is level with the existing floor.

Figure 7. A two-story addition with a hip roof and full foundation that takes advantage of a hilly topography. Framing the second floor is basically the same as framing the first floor, though at first glance the job looks very difficult.

Figure 8. A hip roof abuts a straight wall. Foundation is crawl space.

Figure 9. A full foundation allows two stories to be added —a garage and room above.

Figure 10. A shed-roof addition in line with a gable-roof house. Foundation is a crawl space.

Figure 11. In this type of situation, a different kind of roof other than the flat roof illustrated would have been very complicated. To determine the construction elements to be used in your addition, examine many different additions; people who draft plans also suggest the best approach to take.

Figure 12. A two-story addition with a gable roof that intersects a sloping roof. The addition has been put on a slab foundation and the floors of the addition and the existing house are level.

Figure 13. A corner is often a good spot for an addition.

Figure 14. That corner filled—with plenty of new space.

HOW TO
ADD A ROOM
TO YOUR HOUSE

Figure 15. The authors' addition: a shed roof intersecting a straight wall.

CHAPTER **1**

Building an Addition: Basic Considerations

Before you begin to build an addition, there is a grab bag of things to consider and some things to do.

ATTITUDE AND ALTERNATIVES

Perhaps the most basic thing of all is to examine your attitude: namely, will you enjoy the work? If you don't think you will, think twice about doing it. Construction can take many months and create a mess; if you won't enjoy the project, it can become quite tiresome.

Of course, you can decide that you won't enjoy it that much, but still want to do it because of the money you'll save. And you can save a lot. For an average room addition, by doing it yourself, you will save one-half to two-thirds of what you might pay a contractor.

You also should consider whether extending your home is preferable to moving. There can be any number of reasons for extending your home. It may be that not moving is important to your work; you may have low taxes and mortgage payments that would increase if you moved; you might disrupt the lives of your children by moving; or, perhaps, mortgage money for a new home is difficult to obtain.

You should know, too, that you may be able to gain the space you need by other, simpler means. Adding a dormer in the attic is one way. It can increase headroom and, therefore, usable floor space. Other possibilities are converting the garage to a room, finishing a basement or attic, or simply dividing existing rooms with partition walls.

LIMITATIONS

The town in which you live will have restrictions as to where on your property you can build the addition. In general, you can't add to the front of the house because this would constitute an encroachment on town property. A possible exception: you have an L-shaped house with one leg of the L facing the front. You may be able to add to the front (inside the juncture of the L) as long as you don't go beyond the leg. Usually you'll be restricted on adding to the sides of your home as well. Generally, adding to the back of the house is the best solution, if there is enough property and no restrictions. However, there may be restrictions on the size of the addition you can build relative to the total size of the property.

In some cases, adding to the side or front may be allowed if you obtain a variance—a modification of the law. Getting this, however, usually requires hiring a lawyer, and the red tape one must go through may not be worth it.

LEGAL DOCUMENTS

There are a number of documents you must acquire before building an addition.

Number one is a building permit, which is obtained from the local building-code authorities. To get this, however, you will most likely have to have professionally drawn plans of the addition, and this will require hiring a drafting service or, if the addition exceeds a certain size, an architect. In order to identify your property you'll need the lot and lot numbers. You can get these from a tax bill.

A drafting service in the business of securing permits can be helpful in ways other than by just drawing plans. These people know the personnel at the building departments and know what is required. With their help, you'll be able to go to the building authority with all the correct papers the first time. Their fees are usually moderate in terms of the service they supply.

You may also need a survey of the land. You can obtain this from the company that holds the title insurance. Another document you may be required to have is a certificate of completion.

TAXES

When you build an addition, your house will also be reassessed for taxes, although the amount of increase will usually be modest. The taxes are normally assessed against the entire house and property, not just the addition.

PLANNING

Thorough planning is fundamental to building an addition you will be satisfied with. Undoubtedly, you will have to make compromises, but the idea is to include everything you want to add in your first plan, and then whittle away things based on limitations imposed by size, cost, shape, layout, or taxes.

You should include proposed furniture or kitchen cabinets, as well as plumbing and electrical fixtures. And consider how you will handle the wall that abuts the addition. For example, if you plan to make an opening in it for a doorway, this can be done fairly easily, even in a masonry wall. You simply can enlarge an existing window. On the other hand, if the wall is solid masonry and you want to remove it, you will have to support the wall above, and this is no small problem.

SELECTING LUMBER

When buying lumber for your project, there are a number of factors to keep in mind.

The first is that you should use so-called "green" lumber. This has a higher moisture content than kiln-dried, but it is less expensive.

Lumber is generally broken down into three grade classifications, with No. 1 the best and Nos. 2 and 3 following in quality. A corresponding classification is Construction, Stan-dard, and Utility, which is about the same as Nos. 1, 2, and 3. Each of the grades has a certain strength and other characteristics, which will make one grade more suitable than another. Discuss what you need with your dealer. It is important to buy the material that's just right for the job at hand—not lumber that's too good or not good enough.

Though lumber is graded, and the grade marks are stamped on the pieces, it is best to select boards as if buying fruit. Some will be better—that is, straighter—than others. (A small amount of warpage may be acceptable for some parts of the construction.) Sighting down the board from one end to the other will quickly give you an idea of whether or not a board is warped.

Various types of wood are sold. For an addition, where strength is desirable, only fir or hemlock should be used; fir is the more expensive of the two. There are lumberyards that stock ungraded spruce and yellow pine, but these kinds of wood are not acceptable for the job.

When checking the grade of lumber, make sure the grade marks are meaningful. Some dealers will stamp boards STUD, but it means nothing. Look for the classifications just described.

If you have worked with wood before, you will know that boards have a nominal or named size and an actual size, with the latter smaller. If trends continue, the boards will get even smaller. Below is a table of nominal and actual sizes as they are now. However, when you begin the project check to see if they have changed.

Nominal Inches	Actual Inches
2 x 2	1⁹/₁₆″ x 1⁹/₁₆″
2 x 3	1⁹/₁₆″ x 2½″
2 x 4	1⁹/₁₆″ x 3½″
2 x 6	1⁹/₁₆″ x 5½″
2 x 8	1⁹/₁₆″ x 7¼″
2 x 10	1⁹/₁₆″ x 9¼″
2 x 12	1⁹/₁₆″ x 11¼″
3 x 8	2½″ x 7¼″
3 x 10	2½″ x 9¼″
4 x 4	3½″ x 3½″
4 x 6	3½″ x 5½″

Saving Money on Lumber

When buying lumber, you can save money if you can arrange with your lumberyard to buy it all at once, either paying for it in one lump sum or in periodic payments. You can expect to save about 10 percent. In any case, leave the material at the yard. Unless you have a good place of your own to secure it, it could be the target of vandalism or thievery.

DEFINING TERMS

Throughout the book a number of terms are used with which some do-it-yourselfers may not be familiar. Following is a list of these and what they mean (see also Figs. 16 and 17):

Ceiling Beams. In single-story construction, framing members or ceiling beams are required to secure ceiling material. Unlike joists, which are commonly 2 x 8 or 2 x 10 boards, ceiling beams are 2 x 4s or 2 x 6s. They are not intended to support any weight except ceiling material.

Collar Beams. Collar beams are members that connect rafters. They are secured on pairs of rafters 4 inches apart.

Common Rafter. A common rafter is any rafter that is, as the name connotes, the most commonly used member in roof construction. It extends from the plate to the ridge rafter.

Common Studs. Common studs are the main—or most common—studs (the vertical wall-framing members) used in wall construction.

Cripple Studs. When the area above a window or door is open, it is often filled with very short studs known as cripple studs. They start at the plate and go down to a header but do not touch the shoe.

Facias. Facias are the boards secured to the ends of the rafters or to the top edge of the house as trim.

Footing. The concrete strips upon which the foundation walls or slab edges rest, the footing is physically the lowest unit of the structure.

Full Foundation Wall. The full foundation is one of the main types of foundations. It mainly consists of concrete-block walls that support the

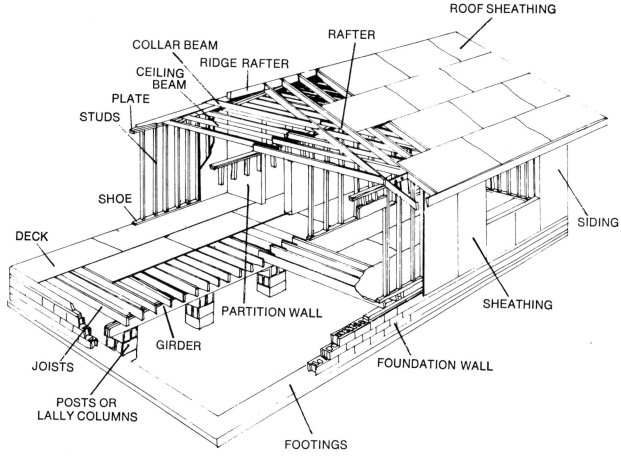

Figure 16. Structural parts of a house.

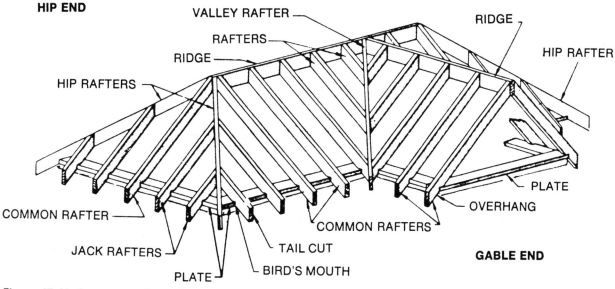

Figure 17. Various parts of a roof.

wood superstructure of the addition (or house).

Grade. Grade is a term commonly used to describe the slope of the ground.

Header. At the top of every door or window there is a solid board, usually very wide and thick, which is called the header. In some cases it has no supportive function, but in others, such as in an arch or large window, it can be a main load-bearing support.

Hip Rafter. Some roofs are constructed so that they bulge upward, and the rafters installed on them are called hip rafters.

Jack Studs. Jack studs are short studs often fastened to common studs. They are used in framing windows and doors where studs shorter than the common type are required.

Jambs. Jambs are the top horizontal and vertical members of door and window frames.

Joists. In construction, joists are used where there is a space underneath the floor, i.e., foundation walls. Their primary purpose is to support the floor; they are the members to which subfloor and finish flooring is applied. In two-story construction, joists are used between floors and are the bottom members for supporting second-story flooring. They are commonly and erroneously called ceiling beams.

Lally. The Lally is a cement-filled steel post or column used to support a girder.

Plate. The plate is the top horizontal member in wall construction. It goes across the top of the studs. It is also made with doubled 2 x 4s.

Ridge Rafter. The ridge rafter may be defined as the spine of roof construction. It is the uppermost rafter, and the top ends of other rafters rest against it.

Screed. To level material with tops of form boards by using a back-and-forth motion is to screed.

Shoe. In wall construction, the shoe is the bottom horizontal member to which studs are nailed. In a slab foundation the shoe rather than the sill is bolted directly to the cement. When foundation walls are used, the shoe is nailed to the subflooring. Shoes are commonly made of 2 x 4 lumber and are doubled when bolted to a slab, but single thickness when nailed to subflooring.

Sill. A board or boards bolted to the top of foundation walls. A sill also refers to the bottom horizontal member on a window framing.

Slab. Another type of foundation, the slab is a deck of concrete set directly on the earth.

Soffit. The board material used to box off the bottoms of the rafter ends is the soffit.

Valley Rafter. In roof construction that involves a roof intersecting a sloping roof, some rafters abut the roof, forming a kind of valley between their bottom ends and the roof, hence the name.

CHAPTER **2**

Foundations

THREE KINDS OF FOUNDATIONS

There are three basic foundations—slab, full, and crawl space—you can use to build an extension, each with advantages in particular situations.

Slab Foundation

A slab foundation is a deck of concrete (there are also footings under the edges) that rests on the earth and upon which all framing members rest (Fig. 18). This type of foundation should be used when the floor framing of the extension is close to the ground. If a floor is installed close to, or directly on the ground, it can be affected by moisture and be subject to

rot or attack from termites. As a general rule, wood should not be closer than a foot from grade.

A slab floor is also recommended if there is an existing slab floor and it is close to grade. If you use another type of foundation, such as a full foundation, you could undermine the existing slab because you'd have to dig down a number of feet (five to seven); this could make the earth under the slab slide out into your excavation.

Another good situation for a slab is where the grade of the house to which you will build the addition runs uphill. To install a slab will require only a minimum amount of soil to be dug from the hilly part.

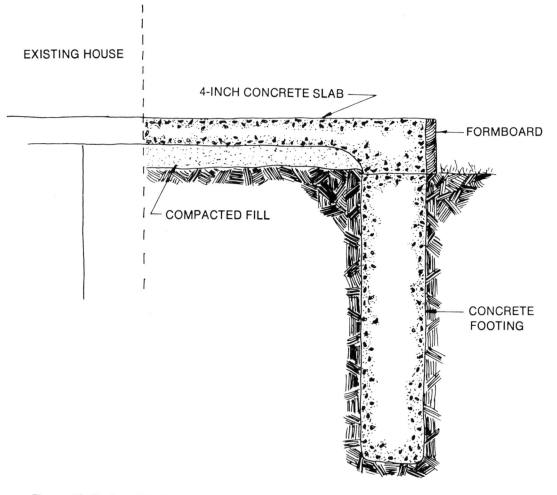

EXISTING HOUSE

4-INCH CONCRETE SLAB

FORMBOARD

COMPACTED FILL

CONCRETE FOOTING

Figure 18. Typical slab foundation.

Full Foundation

A full foundation is one with footings and three concrete-block walls (none is required against the existing house) on top. The wood framework of the addition rests on top of the walls (Fig. 19). In essence, a full foundation is a big hole in the ground surrounded by three walls (and house wall). After the walls (and the extension) are built, a slab floor is poured on the earth.

Crawl-Space Foundation

A foundation with a crawl space is simply one with shorter walls than a

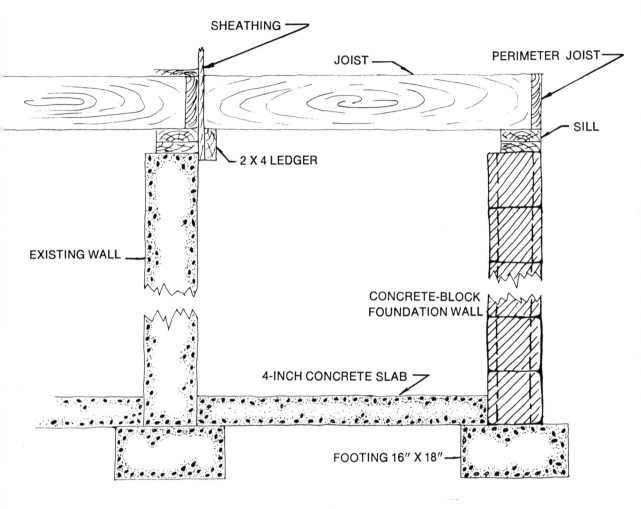

Figure 19. A full foundation showing some members it supports.

full foundation: when the extension or house is constructed, the space under it literally allows room for crawling, but no more (Fig. 20). One situation where you'd want to use either a full or crawl-space foundation is where there is an existing crawl space or full foundation. Here, you just have to dig out to the existing footings and construct the walls to the same height. You won't have to regrade the property. If you used a slab, you'd need soil fill under it to raise it to the level or close to the level of the existing floor, depending on your plan.

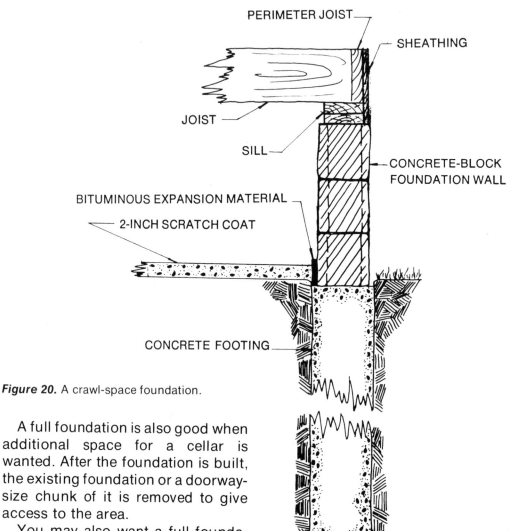

PERIMETER JOIST

SHEATHING

JOIST

SILL

CONCRETE-BLOCK
FOUNDATION WALL

BITUMINOUS EXPANSION MATERIAL

2-INCH SCRATCH COAT

CONCRETE FOOTING

Figure 20. A crawl-space foundation.

A full foundation is also good when additional space for a cellar is wanted. After the foundation is built, the existing foundation or a doorway-size chunk of it is removed to give access to the area.

You may also want a full foundation simply for the soil fill it will yield, perhaps for an unused cesspool or for regarding your property.

A foundation really may be installed anywhere you wish, as long as it does not undermine the existing foundation.

HOW TO BUILD A FOUNDATION

Whether you build a slab, full, or crawl-space foundation, the first step is to outline the foundation on the ground with stakes and string. The main thing is to make sure that the strings are parallel and square to one another (Fig. 21).

You may have the addition planned so one wall is in line with the end of the existing foundation and one wall abuts it. If so, start by extending a string along the foundation wall that will be aligned with one extension wall.

Stake or attach to the house one end of the string (to the back corner of the house) and extend it all the way out past the house and four feet on each side beyond where the exterior wall of the extension will be. If on the existing wall there is an obstruction, such as a chimney or pipe, you may not be able to run the string against the house. In this instance place the stakes (1 x 2s two feet long) so that when you tie a string between them, the distance clears the obstruction and is parallel to the side of the house.

Measure equal distances to points that represent the two outside foundation walls or slab edges that lie perpendicular to the existing house. Secure stakes and tie a string between them to represent the edge.

Using the first line as a starting point, establish stakes and string to

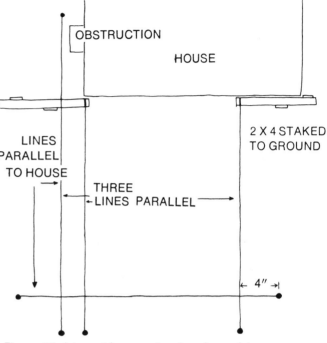

Figure 21. A layout for an extension. A special trick is to nail a 2 x 4 to stakes, as shown. Then attach strings to the stakes for measuring.

outline the opposite edge. Both edges should be parallel.

Next, stake a string parallel to the house wall; the string should intersect and go beyond the first two strings about four feet on each side. Later, when you dig and build, you can remove the strings for convenience, but the stakes will remain, allowing you to reattach strings as needed during the various phases of construction. Note that strings should always run along the outside edges of the proposed foundation.

With the strings in place, check them with a tape for parallel all ways, and also from corner to corner—the diagonals—for squareness. Adjust string positions as required.

If you are marking off an extension where both side walls abut against the house, follow the procedure above, except you usually don't need to worry about obstructions.

Building a Full Foundation

If you are building a full foundation, the best bet is to hire someone with a backhoe to do the digging. This can make relatively light work of a job that will otherwise be very difficult. The excavation should go as deep as the existing footings. At the edges of the hole, where the new footings will rest, the operator should only dig within a few inches from where the top of the footings will go. You want compact, undisturbed earth for the concrete to rest on. Use a square-nosed shovel to carefully remove the last few inches. The depth of the trenches for the footings of any foundation wall must go beneath the frost line for your area (on Long Island, this is three feet). Otherwise, the earth under the foundation can freeze; as it does, it will expand and heave or push the walls up out of position. Your local building code will tell you how deep to go.

To allow room for working, the excavation should be two feet wider at the top than at the bottom of the hole. There should also be a foot of space between the edges of the footing and the walls of the hole. This will allow space for installing 16-inch-wide footings and 8-inch walls. When the terrain is hilly, dig a series of "steps" in the trenches to ensure that all sections of the footings are below the frost line.

Footings for a full foundation can be made with concrete. For this, make forms for the concrete with 2 x 8 boards. The boards should be nailed together at the corners and backed up with earth so they don't buckle when filled. To prevent the earth from caving them in the other way, it's a good idea to insert 1 x 2 boards as spreaders at intervals along the forms (Fig. 22). Make sure the tops of the forms are level. Footings should be located so that the foundation walls will be in the center. If your addition is more than 16 feet long and girders are required, you will need to make footings for the Lallys at this time. (See Chapter Four.)

Once the forms are in place, fill them halfway with concrete and then rocks or, preferably, pieces of a slab you might have broken up (Figs. 23, 24). Using this material will save on concrete. It is important to first soak the rocks or concrete pieces in water (Fig. 25), so they don't suck moisture from surrounding concrete.

Finally, add more concrete and use a board to screed it level with the tops of the forms (Figs. 26, 27).

Cement (not cinder) blocks are used to erect the walls on top of the footing. To locate the first blocks on either wall, replace the strings on the stakes. Following the strings, use a plumb bob or level to mark string lo-

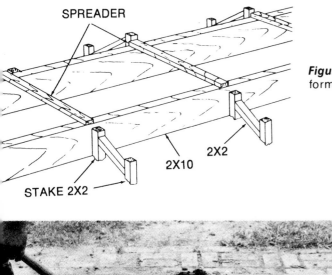

Figure 22. A footing form for full foundation.

SPREADER

2X2

2X10

STAKE 2X2

Figure 23. Use a hoe to mix mortar or concrete. It's best to form it into a pile, making a crater in the center in which to pour water.

Figure 24. Fill form halfway with concrete, then add rocks or pieces of any broken-up slab you may have.

Figure 25. Soak rocks before you place them.

Figure 26. Screed the concrete level with tops of forms, using a board.

Figure 27. Form should be absolutely level and smooth.

Figure 28. First course of block being leveled. Note board under the level—which, in effect, makes it a longer level.

cations on the footings. Also plumb down from the spot where the strings cross above the footing, mark this, then snap a chalkline between all the marks. Mark all sides of the footing and remove the strings.

You can lay the first course of block on the concrete while it is still wet; the blocks become an integral part of the footing (Fig. 28). Or, you can let the footing dry and set the first course with mortar. Solid cement blocks should be used for the top course and hollow-core blocks for all others.

To set the blocks on each wall, follow your chalklines and set a block on each corner of the footing first, then lay loose blocks on top of these and extend strings between them (wrap strings around blocks) as a guide to where the outside edges of the other blocks in each course will go.

On wet concrete, fill the voids in the blocks on the first course(s) with concrete (Fig. 29). On a concrete footing that is dry, lay blocks with about ½ inch of mortar between them.

String guides should be used for subsequent courses; i.e., set loose blocks on corner blocks and stretch strings between them (Fig. 30). As you go, constantly check the blocks with a 4-foot level for plumb and level.

There are a variety of things to observe when installing blocks (Figs. 31 to 39); see advice on pages 21 and 22.

Figure 29. Fill the top of first course with concrete.

Figure 30. Loose block is set on the first course and string is wrapped around it as a guide (along with lines on footing) for placing other blocks.

Figure 31. Corner blocks are established on top of first course.

Figure 32. Half-inch bed of mortar laid on top of first course. Note string guide and block position—blocks are easier to butter this way.

Figure 33. Block being buttered. Mortar should be wiped on firmly so that it can't peel off when block is raised. Don't leave any gaps between mortar and edge of the block.

Figure 34. Block being set in place.

Figure 35. Excess mortar should be scraped off immediately.

Figure 36. A mortar tub (which you can rent) is handy.

Figure 37. A mason's hook is useful for holding string, so that you don't have to wrap it around loose block.

Figure 38. Tap block level with handle of trowel.

Figure 39. Check corners constantly for plumb.

• When preparing mortar for setting the blocks, make sure it is always the same consistency. Otherwise, some blocks will settle (in softer material) while others will not.

• Blocks are thicker on one side than the other. Always place the thicker side up.

• Lay four blocks at a time. Tap each block with the trowel handle so it is even with the string. Scrape off the excess and shake it back in the mixing tub. There should not be any gaps in the mortar. Place the blocks that you are going to lay on end next to the wall. When you are working from left to right, the thick side of the block should face to the right. When you are working from right to left, the thick side should face left. "Butter" the top of the wall and the ends of the block on the ground. Pick up the block with the thick side up and the buttered side toward the block already in place; then set it in place.

• Incidentally, when you order blocks, you'll get some regular blocks and some corner blocks. Corner blocks, which are the same size as the regular blocks, will have one flat end and one concave end; the concave end should face inward.

• Sometimes when laying block you will come to the end of a line with just a tiny space to make up. Here, you can avoid having to cut a small portion of block to fit by careful planning: space the blocks a little farther apart all the way down the line so that there is no small space to fill.

• Block courses should be staggered. That is, the mortar joints should not be in a vertical alignment. To ensure this, lay corner blocks in different directions. This will automatically stagger the blocks.

If you need half a block, you can easily break one in the middle, where the walls are thinnest. Just use a mason's hammer to tap a line all around the block, then rap it sharply on either side. When you use half a block, the joints above and below it will be in vertical alignment. To get around this, cut two three-quarter-length blocks and lay them so that the mortar joint comes in the middle of the half-length block (Fig. 40). On the course above that, use the other half of the first block you broke. On the next course up, you can use the two one-quarter-length blocks (the other parts of the second and third blocks you broke first). If the one-quarter-length block shatters while you're trying to cut it, use a three-quarter-length block instead.

Building a Crawl-Space Foundation

The procedure for installing a crawl-space foundation is essentially like installing a full foundation, except, of course, the block walls will be shorter and no separate form for the footing is required. Here, just dig 8-inch-wide trenches below the frost line. Use a narrow-bladed spade for digging, following the staked strings to know where to start the edges of the trenches. Once the digging gets under way, remove the strings so

Figure 40. To keep block joints staggered you must sometimes break them.

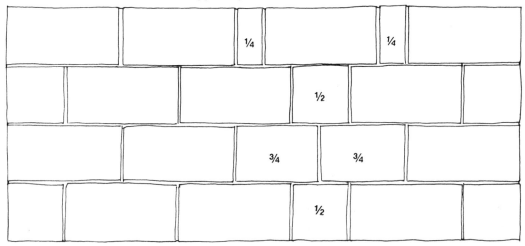

they don't get in your way. Fill the trenches with concrete, then erect the block walls as described for a full foundation. Finally, lay 2 inches of concrete—a "scratch coat"—on the ground inside the walls.

Building a Slab Foundation

There are a few ways you can build a slab, depending on the grade. If the slab is to be close to but above grade, you can install it in one pour of concrete. Excavate to within 6 inches of where you want the top of the slab to fall, and dig 8-inch-wide trenches below the frost line for the footings. Erect 2 x 12 form boards around the perimeter as shown in Figure 45; tops of the boards should fall where the top of the slab will fall. Smooth and tamp the excavated area, fill with 2 inches of bankrun sand. Lay pieces of reinforced wire mesh (6-inch squares) on the sand, propping them up 2 inches, then pour the concrete, filling the trenches, and coming level with the tops of the form boards.

After the pour is made, smooth the surface with a metal trowel, keeping the leading edge of the trowel raised as you make half-moon strokes. The concrete should be made very smooth so that the flooring material will lay flat. If you don't feel capable of this aspect of the job, you can hire a mason to do it. (See Figs. 41–49.)

A high slab—one that is a foot or two above grade—is necessary on a hilly area to keep water from washing

Figure 41. Footing trench for a slab foundation is dug.

Figure 42. A box form is built around stairwell.

Figure 43. All forms must be level.

Figure 44. Concrete is poured.

Figure 45. Rough screeding is done before all concrete is poured. Note section in form removed so wheelbarrow can get through.

Figure 46. Form is full. Smoothing begins.

Figure 47. Smoothing continues. Sometimes a professional is needed to do this.

Figure 48. Finishing touches on the slab.

Figure 49. Slab is poured, ready for framing.

down over it (Fig. 50). Following the procedure previously given, dig 8-inch trenches for the footings. Fill the trenches with concrete, then erect block walls as required.

The slab is poured after the concrete blocks have been set up. Build a form of 2 x 6s around the outside of the concrete-block wall to retain the slab edges. Clean off the top of the blocks with a stiff brush. Fill the voids with metal cans or other material to save on concrete. Do not use wood, because this can attract termites. Fill inside the supports with soil, to within 6 inches of the tops of the forms. Then construct the slab as previously described.

If the slab will be below the top of the foundation walls, the procedure is to excavate, pour the footings, build the foundation walls, build the extension, then come back and break out the existing walls and pour the floor (with access through doors or windows). Normally, footings are 8 inches wide, but in this situation you could make footings that are 12 inches wide, then use 8-inch blocks flush with the outside edge of the 12-inch footing, leaving a 4-inch ledge to rest the edge of the slab on. (See Figs. 51 and 52.)

L bolts should be set on edge of any foundation block or slab while the concrete is still wet. These bolts, about 8 inches long, protrude through the shoe (in the case of a slab), or sill boards (in the case of a full foundation or crawl space), and the sill boards or shoe are slipped over and secured to the bolts with nuts and washers. Place the bolts 1¾ inches in from the edges of the slab or 2¾ inches from the edge of the block wall and a maximum of 12 feet apart, or wherever they'll do the most good in anchoring the framing. Enough of the bolt should be above the concrete (approximately 4 inches) so that it will pass through the boards placed on it.

Under most conditions the foundations described above will be more than acceptable. However, when the ground is not firm enough you have four alternative ways of proceeding:

• Building on pilings. (This is not a do-it-yourself project.)
• Debogging the ground. (Again, it is not practical for the do-it-yourselfer.)
• Compacting the ground. (This requires the services of a surveyor.)
• Using oversize or spread footings.

Your local building-code department should help you in determining if the ground needs special treatment and the best way to proceed.

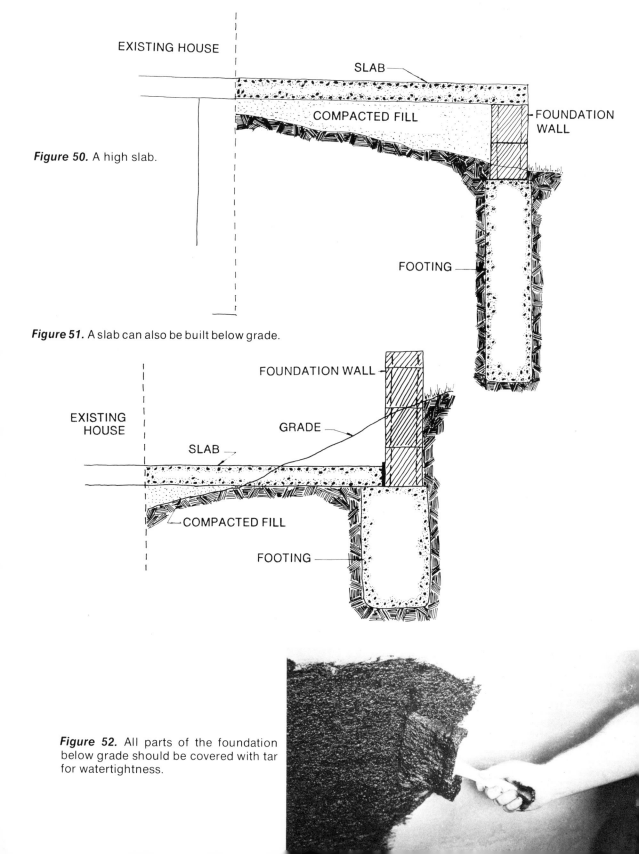

EXISTING HOUSE

SLAB

COMPACTED FILL

FOUNDATION WALL

Figure 50. A high slab.

FOOTING

Figure 51. A slab can also be built below grade.

FOUNDATION WALL

EXISTING HOUSE

GRADE

SLAB

COMPACTED FILL

FOOTING

Figure 52. All parts of the foundation below grade should be covered with tar for watertightness.

CHAPTER 3

Framing: The Sill

After the foundation is in place, the framing members can be installed. On a full foundation or crawl space, the first member is the sill. On a slab the first member is the shoe, but it is made in the same way as a sill.

MAKING THE SILL

The sill is composed of doubled-up 2 x 6s, a nailed-together pair laid on top of each side of the foundation. They are cut so they overlap, and are then secured to the bolts in the foundation.

In installing the sill, it is important to make sure the members are square to one another and to the house. It is entirely possible that the foundation, despite careful effort, will not be exactly square. If the sill is square, however, all of the subsequent framing members that go above can be squared off it.

Fir or hemlock, as mentioned, may be used for the sill members. Select boards as straight as possible.

First, mark the foundation wall where the sill members go, and snap a line 5½ inches (the width of the sill boards) back from the front edges of the foundation on all sides to within a few inches of the house walls. Measure between the lines at the front of the foundation and near the back to see if they are equal distances apart—parallel. If they're not, adjust the lines—strike new ones that are.

Use a measuring tape to check the lines diagonally corner to corner for squareness. Adjust lines as needed. Usually you won't have to adjust the outside points more than ¾ inch to establish square.

Cut the sill boards according to your marks using 2 x 6 stock, a pair of 2 x 6s for each member.

As mentioned, sill members overlap at the corners, the amount of overlap being equal to the width of a 2 x 6 (5½ inches, actual size). Use a scrap piece of 2 x 6 to mark the ends of the longer boards to locate positions for the ends of the shorter boards.

Next, assemble pairs of boards, placing them so the crown, or high sides, face opposite directions. It's best to nail the ends together first so that the sides are even, then toenail through the edge of the boards at the point of greatest crown, to pull them together (Fig. 53). This will tend to straighten both. Finally, nail the boards together on the faces, placing nails 10 to 12 inches apart and staggered from side to side.

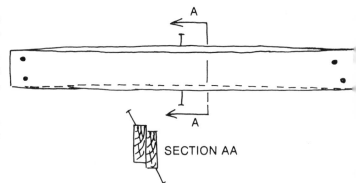

Figure 53. Sill members should be nailed together at the ends, then toenailed at the point of highest crown. This view, of course, is highly exaggerated.

Figure 54. Three-quarter-inch holes are drilled in sill members so they can be slipped over bolts in foundation.

SECURING THE SILL

To secure the sill, follow this procedure for each side:

Lay each sill member in position on the foundation next to the bolts. Use a square to mark on the member where each bolt hole will fall. Measure from the chalkline to the center of each bolt, then make X's on the member where the points are. For example, if the bolt is 2¼ inches from the chalkline, make an X on the member at this point on the board; if another is 2¾ inches, make an X on the board there, and so forth.

At each of these points drill ¾-inch holes (Fig. 54). This is slightly oversized for the bolts, but the small

Figure 55. Use hammer to tap termite shield down around bolt.

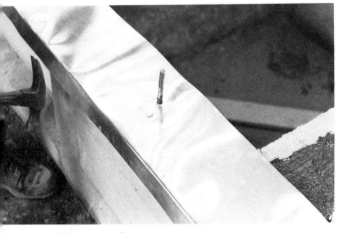

Figure 56. Completed job.

Figure 57. A trick for pre-forming the termite shield before placing it on the foundation is to form it over boards the same width as the foundation.

amount of play is necessary, because it is highly unlikely that one can make the marks perfectly. Try each member to make sure it fits, and lay it aside.

Before installing the sill, it is a good idea to install a termite shield on top of the foundation. This is a strip of aluminum that prevents termites that crawl up the foundation wall from getting into the wood. Stock aluminum (available at lumberyards) that comes in 10-inch-wide rolls is used for this. The material can be bent and cut easily with tin snips.

To add the shield, first check the top of the foundation to make sure there are no holes in it. If there are, fill these with cement and trowel smooth.

Then, on each side, follow this procedure: cut a piece of aluminum 4 inches longer than the side. Align the strip over the bolt holes, pull taut, and use a hammer to tap the aluminum so the bolts punch through it (Figs. 55, 56). Push the strip down so it rests on the foundation; since the foundation is 8 inches and the aluminum 10 inches there will be a 2-inch overlap on the outside. The corner should be overlapped completely. After all the aluminum pieces are cut and fitted over bolts, remove the pieces. (See Fig. 57.)

On any side, use a trowel or an old shingle to apply a ⅛-inch bed of roofing compound (asphaltum) (Figs. 58, 59). Then lay the aluminum on the foundation, snaking the bolts through the holes, embedding the strip firmly in the compound. Repeat on the other sides, also applying compound where strips overlap. Finally, bend the edges (the 2-inch overlap) down so it is not in the way when you install the sill. The back edge is bent up after the sill is unstalled.

Next, slip sill members over the bolts onto the foundation (Figs. 60, 61). Nail the corners together but don't tighten the bolts. Later it may be necessary to raise (shim) the sill members up slightly to plumb the structure, and you can't do it if the bolts are tightened.

Figure 59. Even framed areas should be coated on top with tar.

Figure 60. Close-up view of how sill members overlap at corners.

Figure 58. Tar should be applied to the top of foundation before installing termite shield.

Figure 61. Overall view of sill installed.

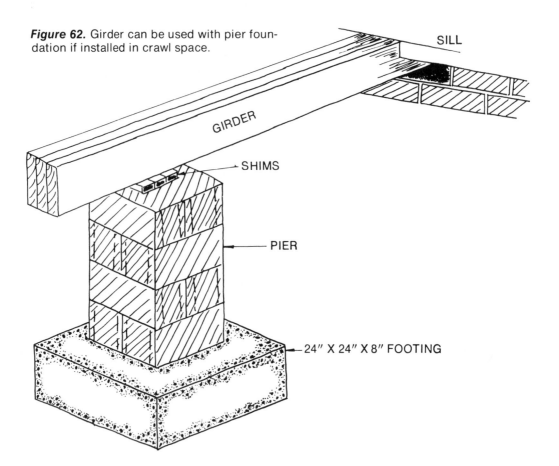

Figure 62. Girder can be used with pier foundation if installed in crawl space.

SILL

GIRDER

SHIMS

PIER

24" X 24" X 8" FOOTING

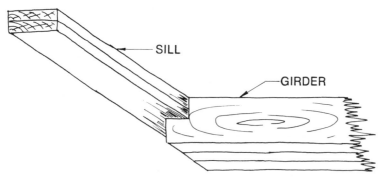

Figure 63. View of girder and sill without foundation.

SILL

GIRDER

CHAPTER **4**

Framing: Girders, Joists, and Subflooring

INSTALLING GIRDERS

Joists are assembled next. But if the addition is more than 16 feet long in both directions, a girder should be used. A girder is a large supporting beam installed under the joists. It can be made of a steel I beam or three 2 X 8s stagger-nailed together. You can avoid using a girder by designing the addition so that it is 16 feet or less in one direction.

The girder must rest on Lally columns (round steel pipes filled with cement with a square plate welded to each end). The Lallys must not be more than 8 feet apart. Each Lally rests on a 24" x 24" x 8" deep footing. Make these footings at the same time as you make the wall footings.

If you are building the addition over a crawl space, you can use cement-block piers instead of Lallys (Fig. 62). Make the piers 16 inches square with two cement blocks in each course. The top of the girder should be at least 4½ inches lower than the foundation wall to allow you to shim up the girder on slate or bricks to make it level.

The end of the girder is cemented into the foundation wall. The easiest way to do this is to leave a block out of the wall and, after the girder is installed, fill in around it with bricks and mortar. Prepare the ends of the members of the girder as shown in Figure 63.

If you are simply going to cut a

doorway into the addition, you have at least 1-inch leeway in the placement of the tops of the sill and girder: a small hump in the doorway won't matter.

The actual size of lumber has been changed many times down through the years, so you simply can't make the foundation of the addition the same height as the old, use all the same nominal-size members above it, and hope to come out at a height where new and old floors will be flush. It takes some calculating.

After the sill is installed, measure the distance between the top of the new sill and the top of the old subfloor. You can see the end of the subfloor by cutting away pieces of siding and sheathing and locating a stud wall on the top of the foundation. Also measure the thickness of the finished floor inside the house by removing the baseboard and inserting a tape measure down along the edge. Next, measure the height of the new joist and the new subfloor, then compensate for the difference between new and old materials, either by shimming up the joists when installed (which is easier) or by building up the floor later.

A typical example of the above would be where the old joists measure 7¾ inches and the old subfloor ¾ inch—a total of 8½ inches from the top of the subfloor to the top of the new sill. The new joists, which are smaller, measure 7¼ inches and the subfloor measures ½ inch, for a total

of 7¾ inches, leaving a difference of ¾ inch. So, add a layer of ¾-inch sheathing to the top of the sill and girder (if there is one) before installing the joists.

To install a girder, start by resting it temporarily on an A frame made of 2 x 4s (Fig. 64). To assemble the A frame, lay one 2 x 4 on the ground next to the footing. Cut two more to form the sides of the A reaching up from the 2 x 4 on the ground to the height of the bottom of the girder. The bottom ends should be 18 to 24 inches apart. The tops are nailed together.

The nailed-up girder will be too heavy to lift, so you will have to assemble it in place.

Rest one end of the center member of the girder in the notch in the foundation and the other end on the top of the A frame. At this point you must have a helper to hold up the A frame. Toenail the girder member to the sill so that the top of the girder is even with the top of the sill and nail into it through the A frame. Raise or lower the end of the girder member to make it level by closing or opening the legs of the A frame. When it is level, nail the lower ends of the A to the 2 x 4 they rest on. This first member should extend from the foundation to the center of the first Lally. The second member is nailed to it and extends from the foundation to the center of the second Lally.

Build another A frame to support the end of this member. The third

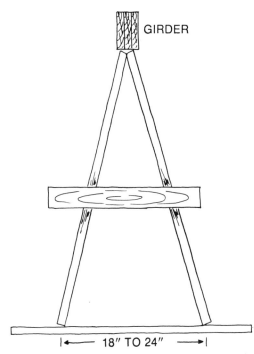

GIRDER

|← 18″ TO 24″ →|

Figure 64. An **A** frame is used to support girder while it is installed.

Fill in under the ends of the girder with brick and mortar as soon as possible.

The Lallys are installed after the addition is framed. Check the girder for level again and measure from the girder to the top of the footing and add ¼ inch (to allow for settling). Have the Lallys made up to this length at an ironworks.

To install the Lallys force them in under the girder, making them plumb in both directions, and secure the tops with four 1½″ x ⁵/₁₆″ lag screws with washers. The bottom of the Lally will be secured when the cellar floor is poured.

If the girder abuts the existing foundation, you can use a Lally right next to it to support the girder, or chip away the top of the foundation to receive the end of the girder. If the existing foundation is cement blocks, it will be easier to chip it away. If it is poured concrete, using the Lally will be easier.

member is nailed to the second member and extends from the end of the first member to the opposite wall (assuming only two Lallys). Then the fourth, fifth, and sixth members are added.

All members should be leveled as you go, and the completed assembly checked for level. After it is nailed up, add a cross member to each A frame to keep the 2 x 4s from buckling. If the girder sags as weight is added to the addition, you can raise it by forcing the ends of the A together, prying the ends with a crowbar.

INSTALLING JOISTS

Joists, as mentioned, are members used to support flooring. If you plan to remove the entire wall between the existing house and the addition, then the height is important because you'll want the old floor to be level with the new.

Laying Out the Joists

Joists may be installed parallel to or at right angles to the existing house. They will usually span the foundation in the shortest direction. Use 2 x 8s 16 inches o.c. (on centers) up to 14 feet long and 2 x 8s 12 inches o.c. or 3 x 8s 16 inches o.c. up to 16 feet long.

Sagging

In some cases, the existing floor will have sagged and you will want to ensure that the edge of the extension floor will follow the irregularity. You don't want an annoying bump between floors. (If you are just making a doorway in the existing wall, you won't, as mentioned, have to worry about this. As much as an inch variance in floor heights is permissible.) To solve the problem, you can temporarily nail a 2 x 4 ledger and the house ends of the joists in place, and continue with the construction of the addition until you can remove the wall. When the wall is out, you can remove the ledger strip and raise or lower each joist separately to bring them in line with the existing floor. Then hang each on a sheet-metal joist hanger (Fig. 65).

The joists, as mentioned, should be spaced 16 inches o.c. (12 inches o.c. in the case of 16-foot 2 x 8s). Mark them out on the sill with a framing square. The first joist is moved over so that its center is 16 inches (or 12 inches) from the edge. Make a mark 15¼ inches (or 11¼ inches) from the end of the sill; put the X beyond the mark. Mark out 16-inch centers all the way across the

sill. If you have a girder, mark it the same way. Mark the joists on the opposite wall the same, but put the X on the other side of the mark (Fig. 66).

If your plan works out so that the joists are at right angles to the house, a ledger strip is used. Use a 2 x 4, transferring marks to it from those on the sill. The ledger strip will be shorter than the sill because it will fit between foundation walls.

When laying out the joist locations, put in a double joist under parallel partitions or two joists flanking a partition that will house the plumbing stack, if any (Fig. 67).

If joists are at right angles to the house, start by striking a line the thickness of a 2 x 8 back from the outside edge of the sill (this thickness will allow space for securing a perimeter joist later), then snap a chalkline across the house that is aligned with the top of the sill members (or the shims on the sills, if any) abutting it. Nail the ledger strip to the house with its top edge on the chalkline.

Determine if the house is straight. To do this, stretch a string parallel to the house, and measure the distance from the house to the string at various points along the line.

If the house is straight, measure the distance between the line on the house wall and the sill. Cut one joist to this length. Hold it in place to check it. If it is okay, use it as a template for cutting all the others.

Proceed to mark the joists one by

Figure 65. Joists hung with sheet-metal hangers. Existing floor has irregularities.

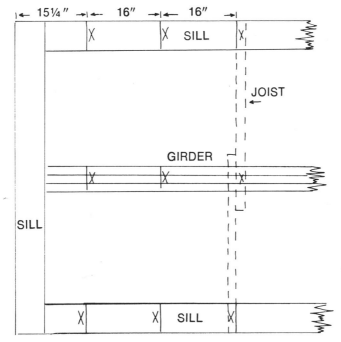

Figure 66. Layout of joists.

one, using this template. One end of a board will usually be square and/or better than the other. Align the good end with the end of the template and mark the other end.

After you have marked all the boards, cut them. (Have a helper move them out of your way as you cut them.) When all are cut, install them crown side up; that is, sight down the joists to determine which is the high side and put this on top. Then, when flooring and other members are installed, the joists will be pressed down straight. The joists should be toenailed to the sill, the house wall, and the 2 x 4 ledger strip, using 10d nails (Fig. 68).

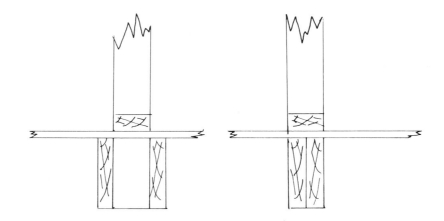

DOUBLED JOISTS UNDER PARTITIONS

Figure 67. Joists should be doubled under parallel partition wall or flank the wall if plumbing stack has to pass through.

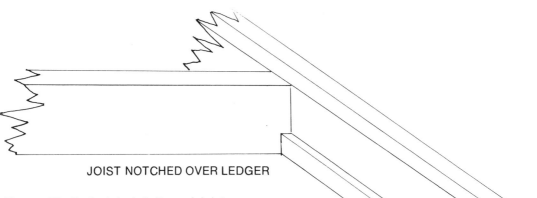

JOIST NOTCHED OVER LEDGER

Figure 68. Typical installation of joists on ledger strip (at house wall).

In instances where the house is not straight—it may be bowed or wavy—it will be necessary to cut each joist individually to the correct length.

Finally, secure a perimeter joist to the ends: simply cut it to fit, lay it across the ends, and nail it home with 10d nails (Fig. 69).

If the joists are parallel to the house, snap lines that are parallel and a joist thickness in from each edge of the side sill members. These lines should be parallel.

Proceed to mark off joists on 16-inch centers. Cut a template joist, cut the joists, then install them according to your marks, toenailing them (10d nails) to the sill. Finally, add perimeter joists around them.

Figure 69. View of how joists are attached from interior of foundation.

Bridging

Bridging is intermediate bracing used on joists over 10 feet long. It is intended to distribute large local loads on the floor: for example, the stress of a piano leg resting above one joist will be shared by the two adjacent joists, because the bridging transmits part of the weight from one joist to the next. Bridging also is supposed to keep the joist from tripping (laying over flat) under excessive loads and to help keep end walls of the house straight (Fig. 70).

There are three kinds of bridging you can use:

• *Solid Bridging.* This is made with pieces of the same size material used for the joists (Fig. 71). It is cut to

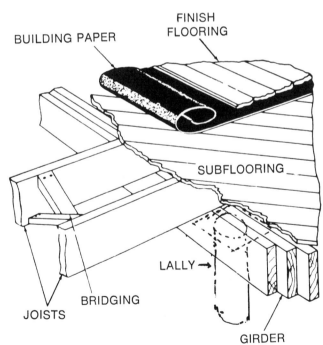

Figure 70. Overall view of Lally column supporting addition members.

fit between joists and nailed in tightly with 10d nails.

To ensure that you get pieces that are the correct length, measure for the pieces at the ends of the joists where the measurements are usually correct; the middle area of the joist is usually incorrect because the joists may not be straight. Solid bridging should be installed between the first and second joists on each end of the extension and above partitions. Toe-nail the bridging to the wall below, and drive nails through the joists into bridging ends. At intermediate points the joists must be straightened be-fore the bridging is nailed to them.

• *1 x 3 or Cross Bridging.* This type of bridging is cut from un-dressed 1 x 3 stock and is installed in between joists in an X shape (Fig. 72). To cut it properly, you should first make a full-size drawing of it to get the proper end angle and length, and then make a cutting jig. Set your cir-cular saw to bevel the ends so they fit the sides of the joists. Also, nail in the tops first, waiting until the finished flooring is down before you nail in the bottoms; the flooring helps to straighten the joists, but if bridging is nailed solid, the joists won't bend.

• *Metal Bridging.* These are thin strips of metal forged for extra rigid-ity and secured to the top edges of the joists. If you use this type of bridging to have a flat floor, then you'll have to notch the joists (using a hatchet) so the ends will be flush with the top edge of each joist.

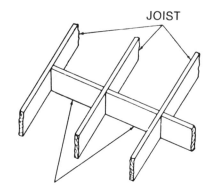

Figure 71. Solid bridging.

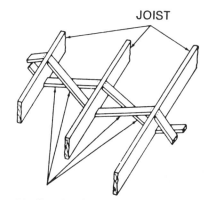

Figure 72. One-by-three or cross bridging.

Solid bridging is desirable where the joists are close together. Metal bridging is more convenient than 1 x 3 because it comes ready-made, but it is harder to install (the joists have to be notched), unless you can tolerate the bump in the floor. One by three is easiest to nail in place but hardest to adjust the length for joists that are close together.

INSTALLING SUBFLOORING

After all joists (except the one next to the house) are nailed in place, nail on the deck or subflooring (Fig. 73). Use ½-inch plywood sheathing. It is a good idea to strike a chalkline across the joists 4 inches from the outside of the box. Use this line to keep the first row of sheathing straight. Start the first course with a full panel (4 x 8) and cut the first pieces of subsequent courses 64 inches and 32 inches to stagger the butts (Fig. 74). Use 6d common nails spaced 7 to 8 inches apart.

Other types of subflooring may be used. For 1 x 4 square-edge subfloor, 1 x 6 tongue and groove, or 1 x 8 shiplap, start at the house end and work out. Use two 8d common nails in each board in each joist. Don't force the boards up tightly; if you do, they will buckle if they get wet. Let the boards overhang the end joist. Don't nail the end joists yet, and don't butt more than four 1 x 4 or three 1 x 6 or 1 x 8 boards in one place on one joist.

Always start with your longest boards and work down through each shorter length, moving them over so that the ends of each group extend past the joists and butt on the first or second joist from the previous butt. Let the final board extend over the edge, but just tack it in place.

Strike chalklines along the three edges even with the outside edge of the perimeter joist. Then cut along this line with a circular saw. This will make the ends straight even if the end joist is not. Align the end joist with the cutoff subfloor and finish nailing.

Figure 73. Partially installed decking.

24″ X 96″	24″ X 96″		
48″ X 32″	48 X 96″	48″ X 96″	
48″ X 64″	48″ X 96		
48″ X 96″	48″ X 96″		

Figure 74. Typical layout of decking. Pieces should butt on joists. If you cut first piece (4 x 8 panel) into 48″ x 32″ and 48″ x 64″ pieces, the other pieces will be staggered automatically and there will be no waste.

CHAPTER 5

Framing: Installing Shoes and Making and Cutting Other Members for Assembly

INSTALLING SHOES AND PLATES

After the deck is completed, the shoes and plates are installed. Once the shoes and plates are in, you can mark them for stud locations, and in turn, use these to mark ceiling beam and rafter locations and second-story joists, if your plan calls for them. Do as much of the layout on the deck or ground as possible, using one set of marks as a guide for making others.

Before you do anything, however, check the deck for squareness. It should be square but if it is not, make sure that the shoe will be. As long as it is square, other members installed on it will be square.

Follow this procedure to install the shoe:

1. Strike lines parallel to and 3½ inches (the width of the 2 x 4 used for shoes) from each edge of the deck (Fig. 75).

2. Check the lines for square—measure diagonals—and adjust them if necessary.

3. Use 10d common nails to secure a 2 x 4 aligned with each of the lines. Cut away just enough of the siding to allow the ends of shoes to butt against the old sheathing.

4. Following your plan, strike lines to locate each partition wall. Each of these should represent one edge of the shoes used, which are also 2 x 4s. Secure with 10d nails, staggered and about a foot apart. Nail into joists wherever possible.

Figure 75. After deck is complete, strike chalkline on it for placing the shoe.

5. In the case of a slab foundation, the procedure is slightly different. Here, shoes should be drilled for the foundation bolts. The procedure is the same as for installing the sill on top of a foundation wall, except you use double 2 x 4s. Also a good idea: Use a termite shield under the shoes.

6. Mark the shoe for all doorway widths, allowing 2 inches more than the nominal width for all interior doorways and 3 inches for exterior doorways. Use a circular saw to cut the materials.

Using the shoes as a guide, cut wall-plate members as indicated so the corners are half-lapped. Tack the bottom members of the plate to the shoes, then install the top members, permanently, assembling plates with 10d nails staggered every foot or so

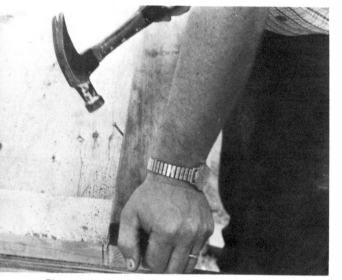

Figure 76. Tack the bottom member of plate onto shoe. Do this on all sides. Leave nail heads exposed.

Figure 77. With bottom members of plates in place, nail top members of plates on permanently. Note how plate members overlap.

(Figs. 76, 77). Do not nail the half-lap corners yet (this is done when the wall is assembled). Leave the plates tacked in place. In the case of a slab foundation, use 2″ x 4″ x 6″ blocks between shoe and plate to make room for the ends of the foundation bolts.

Next, mark locations of studs on the shoes and plates (Figs. 78, 79). You can also mark locations of the ceiling beams and rafters on top of the plate, if you have a one-story extension. If it is a two-story extension, you should mark only the studs and joists, and do the rest of the layout work later.

To lay out for the studs:

1. Following your plan, mark off the location of a rough opening for the windows (the doors have already been laid out). Determine this opening from the windows you are buying; this figure should be in the catalog at the lumberyard, or it should be about ½ inch wider than the overall width of the jamb.

2. Use a framing square to mark the widths of the rough opening on the outside face of the shoe and plate, drawing a line across them. With an *O*, indicate the location of the jack studs on each side of each window and door. Make another line 1½ inches away (stud's actual thickness) and mark an *X* to indicate the location of the common or regular stud.

3. Indicate the location of the corner studs and partition studs. For

corner studs use two *X*'s with a stud space (1½ inches) between them.

4. Finally, mark all the 16-inch centers for the common studs. If you will be using plywood sheathing, make sure that the first studs will be located 15¼ inches from the exterior edge of the corner. In this way, edges of the 8-foot panels will be centered on studs.

To lay out joists for a two-story extension, follow these guidelines:

As the ends of the joists should rest above the studs, draw a squared line across the top of the plate at each stud line.

If a two-story extension is to have a partition wall down the middle, and if the joists are not long enough to span the entire extension—more than 16 feet—then mark plates and partition wall the same as the sills and girder below.

For a one-story extension with a shed roof that intersects a wall, the rafters should rest over the studs. Ceiling beams go alongside them, provided that the top of the original wall has no beam or rafters in the way. In this case, you can move the beams so they rest in a clear area.

To mark locations on the plates for the rafters, extend the lines made for studs to the top of the plate and mark *R*'s there. To mark the ridge rafter, extend the lines you made next to the plate, also marking *R*'s.

In the case of an extension that is

Figure 78. Use a square to draw a line across the shoe and plate members to represent edges of studs.

Figure 79. Draw *X*'s on side adjacent to where studs will fall.

not on the same elevation (i.e., the plate of the existing house and extension are not even), you will have to cut a 2 x 6 nailer to hold the ends of the ceiling beams and another to hold the ends of the rafters.

To make one or a pair of 2 x 6 nailers, simply lay the board(s) alongside the plate and transfer the stud marks to them (Fig. 80). Use an R to indicate the place for the rafter and an X for the ceiling beam (Fig. 81).

If you plan to build a gable or hip roof with an overhang that abuts an existing roof exactly (that is, the facia of the existing house will be continued around the extension), you will have to use the same pitch on the extension as the existing roof. This will make the overhang the same in the extension as in the original, and the valley will work out properly.

On a gabled extension where the ceiling beams will run parallel to the original house and rest on the extension walls and the top of a partition wall, the rafters should be located over studs. If it will abut the wall of the existing house, the ridge rafter should be laid out next to the studs and marked with R's, indicating rafter placement. But if the new roof is going to intersect the existing roof, you can't lay it out at this time.

HIP-RAFTER LAYOUT

If your plan calls for hip-rafter layout, you can also do it now. Looking straight down at your plan, hip rafters travel at a 45-degree angle from walls, and intersect at a point common with the ridge and the common rafters used.

First, mark the center of the plate

Figure 80. Use square to extend lines onto 2 x 6 nailers for ceiling beams and rafters.

that is parallel to the house. The common rafter will rest on and be centered on this mark. Use a piece of 2-inch material to mark the location of the rafter, or make a mark ¾ inch to each side of the center mark. Make an *R* between these marks to indicate the rafter location (Fig. 82).

Next, measure from the rafter to the edge of the wall (distance *B* in Figure 82) and lay it off on both side walls. Put *R*'s on the side of the mark closest to the existing house and an *X* on the other side to indicate ceiling beams, then use the mark to lay out 16-inch centers for the rest of the rafters; rafters will not necessarily fall directly over the studs.

It is not necessary to lay out the ridge rafter at this time, because the rafters lay on 16-inch centers starting at the end of the ridge.

For a two-story extension, make your marks on the second-story shoes and plates.

Figure 81. Mark members where rafters and ceiling beam ends will fall. As you can see, knowing the location of the studs enables you to mark most members from the ground.

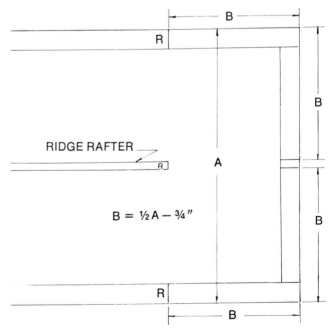

$$B = \tfrac{1}{2}A - \tfrac{3}{4}''$$

Figure 82. Laying out hip-rafter locations.

CHAPTER 6

Framing: Erecting Walls

With the shoe secured and layout work done, you are ready to cut studs, assemble walls, and raise them.

If the new extension is to be the same height as the original one, you should get the length of the studs required from the original house so that the new ceiling will be flush with the existing one.

To do this, open up the wall at some point. Find the top of the plate, measure from the top of it to the top of the subfloor. From this, deduct the total thickness of the shoe and plate. This is the new stud length that you will be required to cut.

If the new extension is not to be at the same level as the original and you want an 8-foot finished ceiling independent of the house, stud length should be 92⅝ inches for a single and 91 inches long for a double shoe used on top of a slab. These lengths will allow for ¾-inch finished floor and a ½-inch Sheetrock ceiling.

Jack-stud length should allow for an 80-inch conventionally sized door with 1-inch clearance above the finished floor. To calculate jack-stud length, compute 80 inches for the door, plus ¾ inches for floor thickness, plus 1-inch clearance, which equals 81¼ inches plus 1¼ inches for the jamb head and horns (protective projections on the jamb). This equals 83 inches above the subfloor; therefore, 83 inches minus 1½ inches shoe thickness equals 81½ inches, the length of the jack stud for a wall with a single shoe and 80 inches for one with a double shoe.

These calculations will make the doors 1 inch higher than conventional practice, but this will mean you will not have to trim doors later to allow clearance for wall-to-wall carpeting, unless it is an extremely high pile and thick padding is used.

It is difficult to make the top of the door jambs higher than 81 inches off the finished floor because 81 inches is the standard length of the jamb. But it may be necessary to make the extension and windows the same height as the existing doors and windows so the exterior trim on the house works out the same.

Count the number of studs (forty or fifty is common) and jacks necessary and cut them to length.

In order to cut all the studs the same, you should build a cutting jib. As shown in Figure 83, nail an 8-foot-long 2 x 4 to an 8-foot-long 2 x 8. Then nail a small square piece of ¼-, ⅜-, or ½-inch plywood to the 2 x 4 on one end. Add a guide strip of lattice (or something of a similar size); its exact placement depends on your saw. Finally, cut and nail a 7-inch 2 x 4 to the 2 x 8 as a stop.

Place two studs at a time in jig with the best end—studs normally have one good and one bad end—of the 2 x 4 against the stop and run the base of your circular saw (Fig. 84) against the guide strip. Remove these two and repeat the procedure as required.

Corner studs can be made next, as detailed in Figure 85. It is important

Figure 83. Stud-cutting jig.

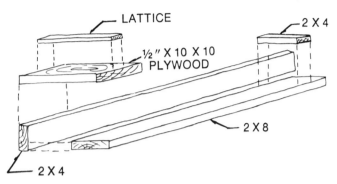

LATTICE

2 X 4

½ " X 10 X 10 PLYWOOD

2 X 8

2 X 4

Figure 84. A stud-cutting jig in use.

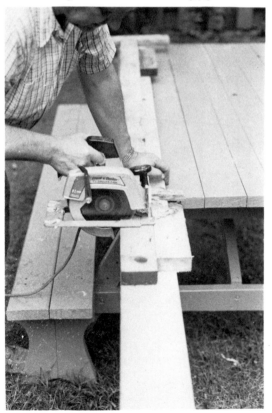

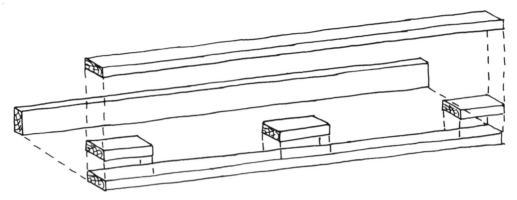

Figure 85. Corner stud.

Figure 86.
Jack stud.

Figure 87. A corner stud partly assembled.

Figure 88. A
partition stud.

to place crowns of the studs in opposite directions to help straighten them. When nailed, studs will be drawn together straight. Nail each jack stud to a common stud (Figs. 86–88).

SECURING STUDS
TO PLATE AND SHOE

In terms of procedure, the studs are toenailed to the plate, then the assembly (one complete wall at a time) is stood up and the studs are toenailed to the shoes. There are other techniques, but this one works quite well.

Clear the deck for action. Label each plate according to its location—east wall, west wall, or wall between the kitchen and dining room, etc.—and remove all plates from the deck except the one for the longest exterior wall.

Lay this plate on edge parallel to and 7 feet from the edge of the deck; marks should be faceup and the plate should be resting on the shoes on either side or on any partition. If the plate is so long it sags in the middle, place a short 2 x 4 block under it for support.

Next, lay the ends of the studs on the marks: a regular stud at each X mark and a stud with a jack nailed to it at the X/O marks, a jack stud on the O mark sides, a corner stud at each end, and partition studs where necessary. So positioned, the studs will overhang the deck about a foot.

The next step is to nail the studs to the plate. Some carpenters can do this by holding the stud against the plate and simply toenailing it on. This, however, takes a lot of practice to perfect. If you have never done it before, it is better to follow this procedure:

Put the stud in position, then put a 2 x 4 block under it and the plate.

Stand behind the plate. While holding the plate down with one foot, and holding the stud end tightly against the plate, lift the stud slightly above the plate and drive a 10d nail through the top toward the plate (Fig. 89). Calculate your "lift" so that when the point of the nail breaks through the end of the stud and enters the plate, the stud face is an ⅛ to a ¼ of an inch above the plate. Then, drive the nail home, pulling it flush with the plate as you do.

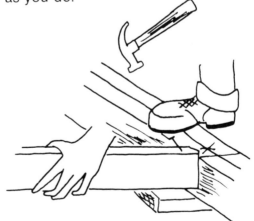

Figure 89. A good method for nailing studs to the plate is to lift the stud above the block and toenail until the nail breaks through with the stud about ⅛ inch above the plate. Final blows will drive the stud flush with the plate.

Figure 90. If stud is too low, toenail through plate as shown to pull it up even.

If the stud ends up too low (not more than ⅛ inch), toenail through the plate into the stud so that it pulls up flush (Fig. 90). If the stud is lower than ⅛ inch, disassemble it and try again.

To complete the securing, drive two more nails through the sides of the stud. Normally, one on each side is sufficient, but it may be necessary to put two on the same side to pull the stud square.

With 10d nails, drive three nails into the end of each stud. You can also use 8d nails if you prefer; in this case, though, use four nails in each stud.

Repeat the nailing procedure for all the studs, as described.

After all studs are nailed in place, cut all the header pieces required. This is simply a matter of measuring between studs, cutting pieces to fit, and nailing them together and then in place. In so doing, keep their faces flush with the outside faces of the studs. To facilitate this, use this trick. Drive a 10d nail into what will be the face of the header near the end (Fig. 91). Repeat the procedure on the other end. Bend the nails over, so you can hang the header on the stud with all the faces flush. Then, stagger the nail through the stud into both ends of the header to secure it. Use five 10d nails on each side.

Next, measure for and cut the ''cripple'' or short studs that go between the top of the header and the bottom of the plate. Secure these on 16-inch centers.

TIPS ON MEMBER SIZES

Header sizes will vary according to where they're being used and the span they must support. The width of

Figure 91. Bent-over nails allow header to hang flush with stud faces.

the header in a bearing wall should be 1 inch more (nominal dimension) than its length in feet. So, a 4 x 6 (made up of two 2 x 6s) header is good up to 5 feet in length. And:

> 4 x 4 is good up to 3'
> 4 x 6 is good up to 5'
> 4 x 8 is good up to 7'
> 4 x 10 is good up to 9'
> 4 x 12 is good up to 11'

This is a rule of thumb and is good for most one- or two-story frame constructions. You could stretch the 4 x 12 to 12 feet instead of 11 feet by picking perfect No. 1 2 x 12s. This kind of lumber is free of defects and gives maximum support. Headers longer than mentioned can be made by adding steel flitch plates between the 2 x 12 members. Consult an engineer for sizes. He will compute the actual strength necessary for a particular job.

Since the jack studs are all the same length, you'll observe that the bigger the header, the smaller the cripple studs. For example, 4 x 10 headers would require 1⅞-inch cripples, while 4 x 8 headers would require 3⅞-inch cripples. Small cripples (1⅞ inches) can be troublesome to nail in—they can split easily. To eliminate this, use a 4 x 12 header.

If you use a 4 x 12 header, the length of the jack studs must be modified. Theoretically, this would be, simply, the length of the stud minus the width of the header. However, lumber shrinks in the yard, and the header can vary in size significantly. What starts out as an 11¼-inch board may shrink to a mere 11 inches. Therefore, it is important to measure the completed header before cutting the jack studs.

A few other points:

• Very large headers are best installed after the wall is raised. You can lift them in place one member at a time.

• Choose a soft, clear, straight-grained 2 x 4 from which to cut the cripple studs.

• After all the studs and headers are in place, nail in the corner posts, toenailing them in place like the studs.

WIND BRACES

Wind braces must be used for extra support if you use certain materials for sheathing: specifically, ¾-inch tongue-and-groove or shiplap sheathing installed parallel to the deck boards, gypsum siding, or any of the new fiber-foam sheathing. You do not need braces when using plywood sheathing or diagonal ¾-inch tongue-and-groove boards or diagonal shiplap sheathing.

The wind brace may be made from 1 x 6 material, either common lumber or a piece of sheathing, and notched or recessed in cuts made in studs, shoe, and plate. Before installing the braces, make sure the studs are straight. The ends of the plate must be even with the shoe under it and each stud must be on its mark. Starting at a corner post, lay the 1 x 6 diagonally across the wall at as close to a 45-degree angle as the construction will permit. Regard doors and windows as the end of a wall; the braces should not pass over these. For a long wall (at least 16 feet) use two braces placed in opposite positions.

Tack the brace in place, then mark where the braces fall on the studs and plate. As mentioned, the brace is also recessed in the shoe. But since the wall is still flat on the deck, you'll have to sight to it and take an educated guess where the brace falls, and mark it, too. Next, remove and lay the 1 x 6 aside and, using a circular saw with the blade set at ¾-inch depth, cut on each mark, then make multiple cuts, about ½ inch apart, between them.

Next, use hammer and chisel to chop out all the little pieces, cleaning out the slots. Use the procedure for all studs, shoes, and plates.

With all slots prepared, lay in the 1 x 6, then nail it to the plate only. You will nail it to other members when the wall has been erected and is plumbed (straightened).

Next, raise the wall. You will need a helper even for a short one: figure one person for every 6 feet of wall.

Before you lift the wall up, lay out material to hold it up, i.e., a 10-foot or 12-foot 2 x 4 for each end or comparably sized piece of 1 x 6 sheathing.

Everyone should stand next to the plate, simultaneously bending and grasping the plate. Raise the wall waist-high, then walk backward until the studs fall off the shoe, then use the shoe as a brace as you raise the plate and swing it up until the wall is vertical (Figs. 92, 93, 94). If done right, the assembly should be on top of the shoe.

With one or more helpers holding the wall up, one person should toenail the corner posts to the shoe (Fig. 95). Then nail braces from the posts to the deck to hold the wall in position. The next step is to toenail the studs to the shoe (Fig. 96).

To ease this job, follow this technique for each: using your foot as a brace behind it, hold the stud off the mark on the shoe about ½ inch (Fig. 97); drive the nail into the stud from the opposite side, gradually knocking it flush with the line. When this is done, drive other nails in (use a total of three 10d or four 8d nails). Many studs have a gentle "licorice" twist shape in them and these nails can be used to correct the condition.

Next, cut a channel in the siding where the side walls will abut the house. See page 65 for instructions. For each wall, nail a stud plumb in this channel.

With one wall up, install either of the ones that abut it. For an easier job, the end of the plate closest to the erected wall should be raised first

Figure 92. Wall assembly should overhang deck as shown, before raising.

Figure 93. The wall assembly is then pulled back and lifted until bottom ends contact shoe.

Figure 94. Push up wall assembly so it rests on shoe.

Figure 96. Toenail stud from opposite side. Hammer blows should drive the stud closer and closer to line.

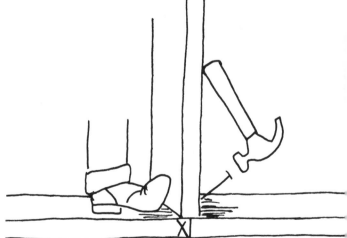

Figure 95. Brace wall assembly in place with 1 x 6 or other material.

Figure 97. Brace the stud with the foot as shown, when toenailing.

and moved over the erected one. To secure each of these walls, follow this procedure:

Raise the wall, then toenail the end of the plate to the house sheathing above the plumb stud already nailed to the wall. The heads of the nails should be left out so the nails can be pulled later. Join the outside corner with three 10d nails.

Loosen the brace, and check the corner for plumb. If it is plumb, nail everything up tightly. If the outside walls lean out too much, nail the half-lap together and trim the plate at the house end to compensate. If the reverse is the situation—the wall leans in (the house wall can lean in, too)—nail the house end up tightly and spread the half-lap to compensate before nailing it together.

Follow the procedure detailed above for all the walls, both outside and partition type.

PLUMBING UP

After all the walls are nailed up in place, it will be likely that only the outside corner posts are plumb, while the long wall is not completely straight. Check. If it's not, it should be adjusted, because you won't be able to plumb anything once additional joists (if a two-story extension) or beams are in.

To plumb, construct a special plumb stick. Select a straight 2 x 4 stud. As shown in Figure 98, nail a 1″ x 2″ x 6″ block to the top end, a 6-inch piece to the other end, and a 6-inch piece to the end grain. To use the stick, simply hang it on the plate, holding level on the stick while keeping the blocks tight to the plate and shoe.

You should plumb all corners in both directions with the plumb stick and level. It's a job for two people. One person uses a level and stick while the other secures bracing (from inside, sheathing goes outside) to bring the offending members to plumb. To brace, first nail the end of a 12-foot 2 x 4 to the plate. The other end rests on the deck. The corner can be forced out by prying with a crowbar on the low end of the 2 x 4 brace. One person should direct the other (with crowbar) until a plumb reading is reached on the level, then the brace is nailed securely. The crowbar technique is effective when the wall is leaning in. If the wall leans out, it can be adjusted by using a temporary brace from the outside.

LONG SPANS

Plumb all corners and all intersecting (partition) walls. When you're finished, the corner posts will be plumb, but other studs may be out.

Use braces as shown in Figure 99. Use the plumb stick (Fig. 98) to determine where the wall is most out of plumb and nail the brace there. If the wall is out near where there is a large header, you can extend a brace from

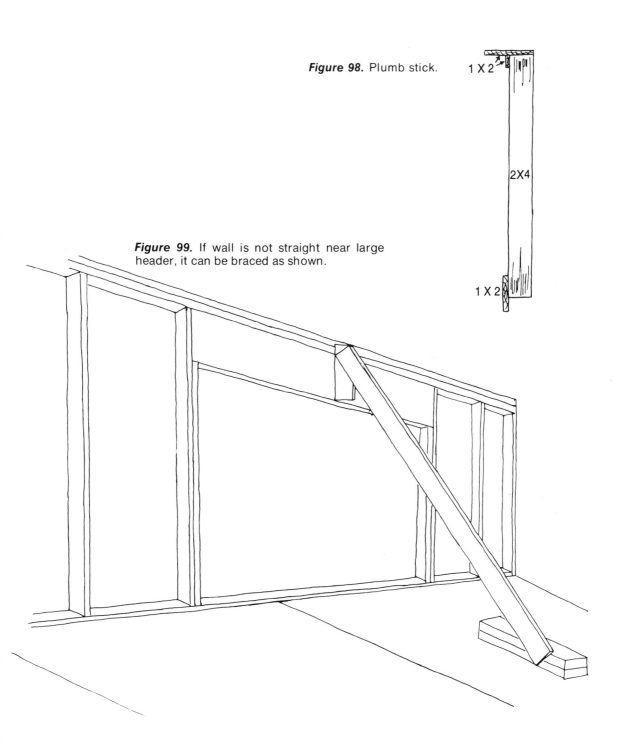

Figure 98. Plumb stick.

1 X 2

2X4

1 X 2

Figure 99. If wall is not straight near large header, it can be braced as shown.

the header to a pair of 2 x 4 blocks secured to the deck. When finished, sight down from one end of the wall (do it from a ladder) to make sure the wall is straight.

After plumbing walls, nail the wind braces on securely, using two 8d nails per slot.

WINDOW FRAMING

When the walls are up, you can frame out the windows, which already have the headers in place. The first step is to determine the height of the rough opening that the window fits into. On new units, the rough opening would probably be listed in the catalog at the lumberyard. If not, it should be calculated as being ½ inch more than the jamb height.

To make the opening, measure down from the bottom of the header and mark the distance on the jack studs.

Cut a 2 x 4 sill to fit between the jack studs. Lay the 2 x 4 on top of the shoe and (using the square) transfer the stud marks (X's) to the sill (Fig. 100). Keeping the sill on the shoe, measure from the top of it to the marks on the jack studs. This will give you the length of short jack studs needed under the sill.

Cut as many short jacks as needed. Remove the sill and toenail the studs to the marks on the shoe. Place sill on stud ends, then nail through it into the ends. Finally, toenail the sill to the regular jack studs.

If the window opening is longer than 5 feet, it is a good idea to double the sill for strength.

SHEATHING

The sheathing is installed next (Fig. 101). The kind you use is determined in part by the siding to cover it, as well as cost. Gypsum sheathing is not recommended, as it is too hard to nail siding to. Different kinds of composition sheathing are suitable, such as Celotex and urethane foam (good for use under brick for insulating value); ¾-inch tongue and groove or shiplap will yield the straightest walls. If you have a long blank wall, wooden sheathing works well. Plywood is the fastest to install, but it's also the most expensive.

When installing sheathing, there are a number of things to remember. For greater strength, plywood sheathing should be installed horizontally rather than vertically (Fig. 102). The plywood should cover the joists, shoes, and sills. Also, apply the material in large sheets. Less nailing is required. Tongue and groove installed diagonally rather than horizontally is stronger but is wasteful and takes longer. If you put it on diagonally, you don't need wind braces.

• Apply sheathing up to about a foot from the plate.

• Any sheet sheathing is best cut to size first, then nailed on.

• Board sheathing should be

Figure 100. Windowsill (in this case a double member) can be marked for its studs by transferring marks from shoe.

Figure 101. Sheathing being installed.

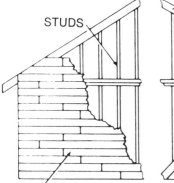
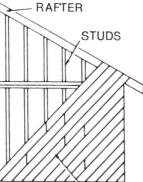

STUDS — RAFTER

STUDS

WALL SHEATHING NAILED
ON HORIZONTALLY

WALL SHEATHING NAILED
ON DIAGONALLY

Figure 102. Diagonal and horizontal wall sheathing.

nailed on and then trimmed in place.

• If you put board sheathing on in small pieces, you can only butt three in a row on studs and then move over. Nail three or four pieces at a time, then trim. Use scrap where it fits.

• For ¾-inch sheathing or tongue and groove, use 8d nails, two to 6-inch board; three to an 8-inch board. For plywood (up to ½ inch) use 6d nails, 8 inches apart. For composition sheathing—2-inch galvanized roofing nails.

THE SECOND FLOOR

If the extension is to be two stories, the time to begin work on the second floor is after you have plumbed up the walls of the first floor. In terms of procedure, you are in the same relative position as when you installed the first-floor sill. The joists should be placed in the same direction and positions as the first-floor joists, except that since the top of the plate is only 4 inches nominal (3½ inches actual) width, instead of the 6-inch sill, there won't be enough room for perimeter joists. Therefore, the ends of the joists must be cut flush to the plates.

The first step is to consider how to hang the joists on the house.

If the joists will be parallel to the house, choose the straightest 2 x 8 you have and nail it to the sheathing (remove siding only in the area where the joist will go) so that its ends rest on the side-wall plates. Cut and secure other joists 16 inches apart. If the joists must butt the existing house, remove siding and strike a chalkline aligned with the tops of the plates. Then secure the nailer you made when you laid out for the joists. To this, secure joist hangers (Tecos) at all the *X* marks. Check the distance from this nailer to the outside of the extension wall at each end and several places in the middle. If distances are all the same, cut all the joists to their marks. If they are different, use the same method detailed for the first-floor joists, and nail them in place.

Special note: It is important that the first-floor walls be plumbed and straightened before the joists are nailed in. Once they are, it will no longer be possible to move the walls.

MAKING CHANNELS FOR SIDE WALLS

To clear siding for the ends of side-walls, first draw a plumb line on the siding ¼ inch beyond where the edge of the new sheathing will fall. The sheathing may be ¾, ⅜, or ½ inch thick, depending on what you use. Then, make a channel for the end of the wall. How you do this will depend on the siding.

• For asbestos shingles, remove all shingles that the plumb line crosses and all shingles whose ends fall in the way of the studs. The shingles can be smashed with a hammer.

• For wooden siding over sheathing, such as clapboard or novelty siding, cut along the line and another 6 inches inside of it. Your saw should be set to a depth where it only cuts siding, not sheathing.

If the wall is to be removed completely, cut through the sheathing at a point just short of where the inside edge of the stud will be. This will allow you to leave the wall relatively intact until the extension is complete.

Cutting a Channel in Brick Veneer

If you wish to keep the veneer intact—you're not knocking the wall out—first draw a plumb line at the outside edge of where the new stud will be. To anchor the first stud, use expansion shields inserted in holes drilled in the mortar lines.

If you wish to remove the wall or just the veneer inside the extension, you'll have to remove it all the way to the top. You can't remove just a bottom portion and leave the top portion (as in the case of a two-story house with a one-story extension) because the bottom bricks support the ones above.

First, draw a plumb line ¼ inch beyond where the edge of the new sheathing will fall. Score this line with a hammer and chisel, then break the veneer with a sledgehammer. It's best to start 2 or 3 feet away from the scored line and work up to it gradually. Once you make a hole in the wall, the bricks will break out more easily. As you get close to the line, use a small lump hammer and finish with a regular hammer and chisel.

It is important not to break the bricks beyond the line, because if you do, you will have to repair them.

If you want to remove a solid masonry wall, you would be well advised to hire a contractor, because this will require heavy steel beams to hold up the second floor.

Cedar Shingles

Strike a plumb line as noted above. Work from the top down using a sharp utility knife. (A saw shouldn't be used because shingle nails can ruin the blade.) Cut through one shingle at a time, opening up a 6-inch channel.

Hand-split shakes are too thick for

cutting out. Here, you're advised to remove whole shingles that fall under the plumb line.

Aluminum siding can be cut with a metal-cutting circular saw blade or with a shears. Following procedures noted above, make a 6-inch channel working from the top down.

CEILING BEAMS

After the walls are erected, the ceiling beams go in. There is no mystery to their installation. They are laid out and installed the same way as the joists (Figs. 103–106). The only difference is that instead of using bridging, you can nail a 2 x 4 or two or three rows of sheathing across them to straighten them, to space the centers evenly, and to straighten them vertically, since you will not install a floor on them.

In the case of the hip roof, the end beams (next to the plate) are not put in place until after all the rafters are in; otherwise, they would interfere with installation of the rafters.

Figure 103. Ceiling beams are installed just as joists are. Note marks for rafters.

Figure 104. Ends are trimmed for roof clearance. No precise angling is required; just trim them lower than the rafters.

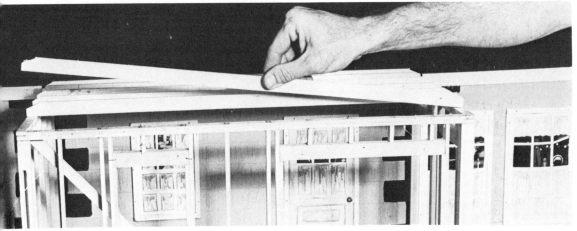

Figure 105. Ceiling beams that are installed parallel to the house are installed here from plate to plate.

Figure 106. Leave the last ceiling beam out on each side. These are installed and nailed to the gable studs after they are in.

Figure 107. A frames are used to support the house while the bearing wall is removed.

CHAPTER 7

Opening Up Walls

After the addition is enclosed, the house wall will be opened up.

Two kinds of walls are used in homes: bearing and partition. The first kind supports a part of the weight of the house, while the partition wall is really just that—a partition. In constructing an addition to your home, your plan may call for the removal of the wall between the house and the addition, and you should determine first if it is bearing. If you remove it without constructing something to take over its weight-holding job, the roof can sag, creating problems you can live without (Fig. 107).

One good way to determine if a wall is bearing is to note if the joist ends, ceiling beams, or rafter ends of the existing house rest on the walls. If they don't, it is not bearing. However, it may become bearing if it will carry the ends of the joists or ceiling beams of the extension.

If it is not bearing, you can remove it whenever you are ready, without further ado. Usually the best time to do this is after the extension is closed in; you don't have to worry about weather.

If the wall is bearing, you must build either an arch (header) or a girder to carry the load, and this should also be done after the extension is closed in. If the wall is going to support more than two joists, you should build a temporary wall to support the weight as you work.

The temporary wall is made of a plate and shoe with 2 x 4s wedged in between them.

Cut the plate—two 2 x 4s—a foot longer than the opening you're going to make. Nail these boards together as you would any plate. Cut a shoe that's at least as long.

Lay the shoe in place (it can go on finished flooring or carpeting) with the plate on top of it.

Measure the distance between the top of the plate and the ceiling. Cut studs this height, plus ¾ inch, plus the distance you figure the floor covering, if any, will compress when the ends of the studs are wedged tightly against it.

Lay the shoe in place, then have a helper hold the plate in place. Use a hammer to wedge one stud in under the middle of the plate, then another at an angle to it. Use a flat bar to pry the bottoms of the studs closer together, thereby jamming the plate tightly against the ceiling to form an A shape.

Proceed to wedge other pairs of studs in place in the same way, making pairs 32 inches on centers. Finally, secure them by nailing (10d nails) them to plate and shoe as needed, leaving the nailheads exposed so you can pull them out as required.

The arch—which is really just a header—may be installed like any other header with cripple studs between it and the plate. If you want maximum head room, install the header flush against the plate.

If you want the ceiling of the extension and existing house to be flush, you will have to build a girder along with your extension (Fig. 108); the girder can also be constructed so that the existing and second-floor extension floors will be flush, as well as the ceiling.

First, remove the sheathing to expose the ends of the joists. In most cases, they will be 2 x 8s or 3 x 8s.

Nail (use 10d or 16d nails) a 2 x 8 across the ends of the joists from wall to wall and then nail two more 2 x 8s to it from the girder. The 6 x 8 girder thus formed is good only up to 9 feet. If the span is longer, you will need a 4 x 4 post under it in the middle. (A 6 x 10 girder is good up to 11 feet, but you won't be able to use it unless the existing joists are 10 inches high, which is unlikely.)

Longer spans can be supported by a flitch plate, a steel plate sandwiched in the girder. But the actual construction must be designed for a particular purpose.

If there is no reason to have the top of the girder flush (there is no floor over it), you can use wider headers instead (Fig. 109).

After the girder is in place, you can nail joist hangers to it (every 16 inches) corresponding to marks on the opposite plate. After the joists are installed, you must cap all the partitions that are parallel to the joists so that you will have something to

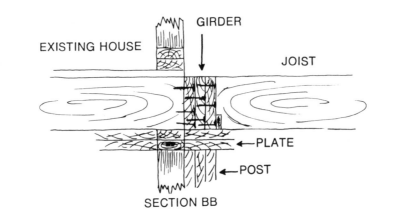

EXISTING HOUSE

GIRDER

JOIST

← PLATE

← POST

SECTION BB

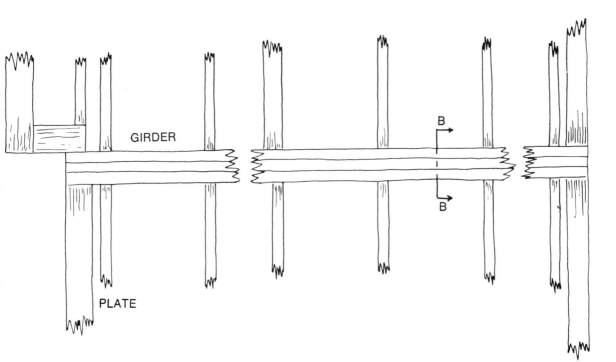

GIRDER

B

B

PLATE

Figure 108. If you want a flush ceiling and the wall is bearing between the extension and existing house, a girder must be built.

which to secure the Sheetrock. Two-inch material will make better nailers than 1-inch material but either, nailed securely, is okay. Use 10d nails. If the partition is flanked by joists, no cap is needed—you can secure the Sheetrock to the joists.

If you want to open up a long span, you may need a steel beam. Another way is to use a method popularly used with Levitt homes. This is an A frame with a turnbuckle supporting a girder up to 20 feet long. Plans are commercially available.

You usually will have to make a compromise when you open up a wall. There are a variety of factors to consider: layout, flush ceiling and floor, cost, your own ability, and so on.

Installing a header in the existing wall is perhaps the best choice. It is the most straightforward method of construction, but this leaves you with the arch. A 4 x 12 header will give you an 11-foot span. In a 16-foot wall this leaves 30 inches on each side. That is quite open.

Figure 109. One way to achieve a flush ceiling.

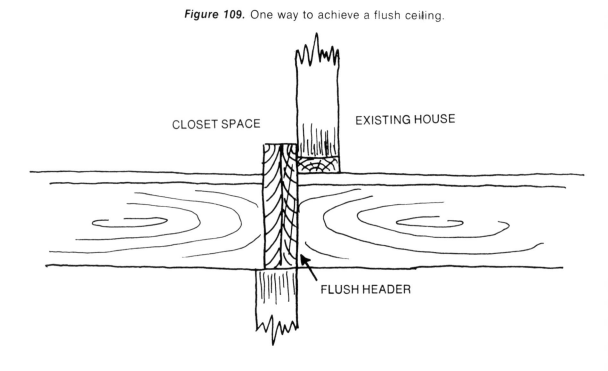

CLOSET SPACE   EXISTING HOUSE

FLUSH HEADER

Figure 110. The header extending under rafters is another way to achieve a flush ceiling.

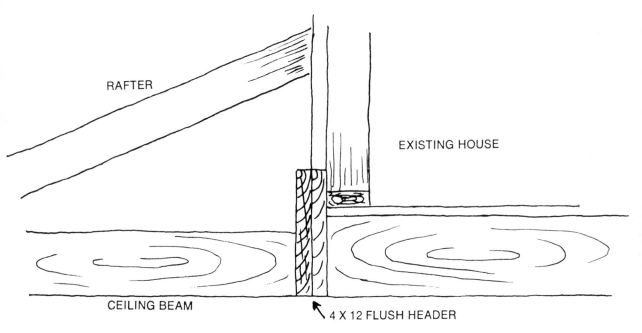

RAFTER

EXISTING HOUSE

CEILING BEAM

4 X 12 FLUSH HEADER

CHAPTER **8**

FRAMING: INSTALLING RAFTERS

You can learn to lay out—measure and cut—all the rafters on the ground with a framing square. (Stanley provides a booklet, with their square, explaining how to use it.)

SETTING UP

Start by first laying some sheathing on the ceiling beams to give you an area to walk on; you should be able to nail both ends of the rafters from this platform.

If you are building a high gable roof, you will need to build a scaffold in the center so you can reach the ridge rafter. In the case of a shed roof you may not know the exact pitch. The plans should show it, but during building you may have to make adjustments. If you are planning to use strip shingles (the regular 3-tab type), the pitch should not be less than 4 inches to the foot (sometimes called ⅓ pitch); 6 on 12 is ½ pitch, 12 on 12 is full.

There are various ways of installing the rafters, depending on what the existing roof is and the type you're installing. Following is a summary.

SHED ROOF THAT MEETS SLOPING ROOF

To lay out a shed roof that meets a sloping one with a 4-inch pitch (4 inches of rise for every foot of horizontal run): choose a straight 2 x 6 to work with. Using a framing square, draw a level line on it as shown in Figure 110. Take this uncut 2 x 6 up on the extension and rest one end on the roof and the other end on the plate. Hold the level on the level line and slide the 2 x 6 up or down the roof, as required, until you get a level reading.

Make sure there are no obstructions in the roof that could be a potential problem, such as dormers, chimneys, stacks, valleys. It might be better to shorten the new roof than build it too close to one of the above. The shorter the new roof, the flatter it will be. This may mean that you will

have to use roll roofing instead of strip shingles.

Use a forked flat bar to remove roof shingles where the end of the 2 x 6 meets the roof, and a strip of shingles where the other rafter ends will fall (Fig. 112). To remove shingles, lift the shingle tab of the second shingle above the one you want to remove. Look for the nail; slide the forked bar under it and the shingle it holds down, and pry up gently about ¼ to ½ inch. Withdraw the bar. Press the shingle down and force the nailhead through the hole in the bar. Pull back and up on the bar and take the nail out altogether. Remove all other nails

Figure 111. The rafter for the shed roof that meets the sloping roof is marked with a level line.

in the same way. Remove the nails in the course below in the same manner and pull out shingles. Once you have these shingles out, the nails that hold the course below will be exposed.

Next, replace the 2 x 6 in whatever location you have decided on. If you have changed the pitch, use a level to make a new level line. Use a piece of scrap 2 x 4 against the end of the 2 x 6 to scribe a line parallel to the roof line (Fig. 113). To do this, hold the end of the rafter on the roof and 2-inch material against it. Draw a line on the rafter along the top edge of the short piece. This line will then be the roof pitch.

Use the framing square to draw a line parallel and a few inches away from the first line if the first line isn't completely on the rafter. This one should cross the board completely. Cut along this line, then nail a 2-inch block of material to the cut edge. This 2-inch piece of material will keep the rafter at the proper slope (it takes the place of the nailer it will be secured to) when you cut it to fit against the plate at the other end. Replace the board and check it for level again.

Mark the lower 2 x 6 where it contacts the edge of the plate.

Use the framing square to mark the bird's mouth where the 2 x 6 contacts the plate and cut it out (Fig. 114).

Again, put the rafter back in place and check it for fit. The sloped end should lie flat on the sheathing, and the bird's mouth should fit over the

Figure 112. Shingles are removed where the end of the 2 x 6 meets the roof.

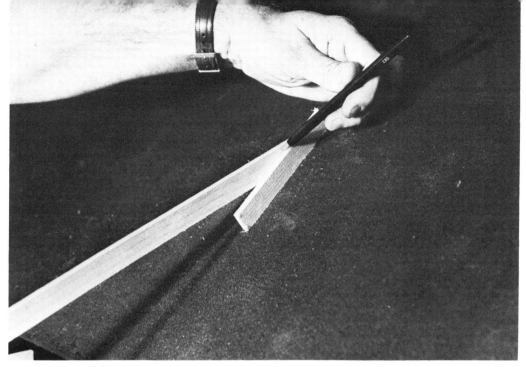

Figure 113. Use scrap board to scribe a line parallel to the roof line.

Figure 114. Bird's mouth has level line and so-called plumb cut. Note dimensions.

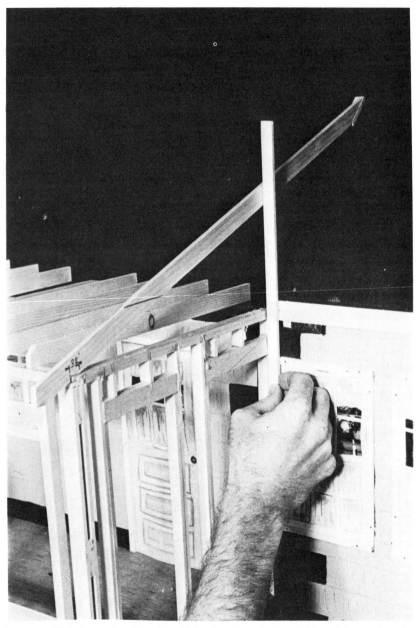

Figure 115. The end rafter should be in line with the side of the extension. Note nailing block on roof end—this block simulates nailer thickness.

plate. In the unlikely event that it doesn't fit, remove it and trim as needed.

When you are satisfied with the fit, use the level to make a plumb mark where you want to cut off the end of the rafter. This will depend on the style of the extension—either flush with the plate or overhang. In this regard, you should know how you will build the soffit because this will affect how you cut the rafter (flush or overhanging). A number of possibilities are shown in Figures 155 and 156.

The cut and fitted rafter will serve as a template for making the other rafters, and also to position the other rafters on the roof.

To do the latter, lay the rafter with nailed-on block in position at one end of the extension and mark the sheathing, where the top of the block falls. Move the rafter to the same position at the other end of the extension and mark. Snap a chalkline across the roof aligned with these marks. This is where the top edges of the prepared nailer will fall.

The end must be in the same plane as the end of the extension (Fig. 115). To do this, sight down from above and move the rafter left and right until it lines up, and mark the roof at the top end of the rafter. Put the end of the prepared nailer on this mark—top on the chalkline—and secure it with 10d common nails (Fig. 116).

Figure 116. Nailer and end rafters in place.

Cutting Other Rafters

The rest of the rafters should now be cut. Like the first, all, of course, are 2 x 6s in this construction.

First, lay all the 2 x 6s on end across two horses with the crowns, or high edges (sight down the boards to determine this), in the same direction.

On each 2 x 6 lay the pattern rafter over it with the top in the same directions as the crowns. Keeping the top edge of the pattern even with the edge of the 2 x 6 at the upper end and at the bird's mouth, mark the rafter for cutting (some 2 x 6s will be twisted; pick out the straightest ones for the end rafters) (Figs. 117–121).

Figure 117. Use straightest boards for end rafters, sighting down to check.

Figure 118. After one rafter is cut, use it as a template to cut others. Wedge keeps boards aligned.

Figure 119. Rafter showing bird's mouth and trimmed overhang.

Figure 120. Plumb-cut end marked (background) and cut (foreground).

Figure 121. Additional rafters in place.

Cut the 2 x 6 on the marks using a circular saw. You will have to cut beyond the corner of the bird's mouth in both directions to get the small piece to fall out. Have a helper move and hold the rafters for you so you can use two hands on the circular saw.

In cutting, the saw guard will be somewhat of a nuisance, but don't tie it back—an unguarded blade is too dangerous. Also, some saws have a lever on the side that you can use to lift the guard if it jams when you start to cut.

When all the rafters are cut, stand them up along the wall of the extension. One person should position himself on the boards laid on the ceiling beams and pull the rafters up as a helper lifts them from the ground.

When they are all up, lay them in position one at a time. Nail the bird's-mouth end in place first, toenailing about the same as on the studs with 10d nails, then nail the upper end to the nailer. Install all the other rafters, aligning them with the *R* marks on the nailer and wall plate.

Gable Studs

The studs on each side of the extension—called the gable studs—may be installed after the rafters are in. Use straight 2 x 4s, in turn standing each up on the *X* marks on the plate and marking them where they intersect end rafters (Fig. 122). Then cut them to this length and nail them in place. When the gable studs are in, you'll be able to install the last ceiling beam on each side. Cut them to fit, place, and then nail to the studs (Fig. 123). See Figure 124.

Figure 122. Gable studs are stood up, marked where rafter crosses them, and cut.

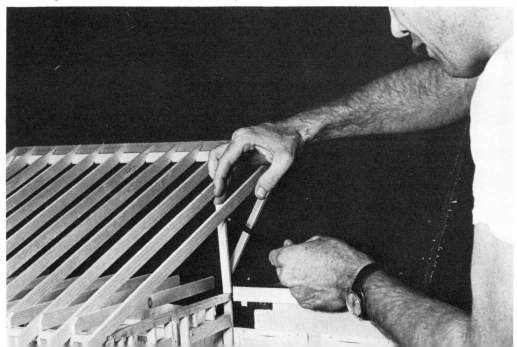

A SHED ROOF THAT INTERSECTS A WALL

When your extension involves this construction, the first thing to do is to nail a rafter nailer to the wall (Fig. 125). You can determine where to locate the nailer mathematically. Simply multiply the width of the extension by the pitch in inches plus 5½ inches (for the height of the rafter).

If, for example, the width (from exterior of extension wall to the house wall) were 10½ feet and the pitch were 4 inches, you'd figure 10½-inch width x 4 inches plus 5½ inches for

Figure 123. When all gable studs are in, final ceiling beam at each end is installed. Nail it to gable studs.

Figure 124. The first step in constructing the shed roof that meets a wall is to nail on the rafter nailer (note rafter ends resting on it). This can be marked on the deck.

Figure 125. Ceiling beams in place.

the rafter height would equal 47½ inches, or the distance from the top of the plate to the top of the nailer. However, the nailer should be at least 4 inches lower than the sill of the lowest window. You could settle for less pitch or you could change a window, if necessary. When the nailer location has been determined, remove the siding along this area. Strike a level chalkline and secure the nailer (2 x 6) to it with 10d or 16d common nails that penetrate the studs. Mark and cut the top of a 2 x 6 so the end fits flush against the nailer. Drive a nail into the end of it and bend it over so you can hang it on the nailer with its top edge flush with the nailer edge. Then proceed to mark and cut the bird's mouth and end. Use this rafter as a pattern for cutting other rafters as described. If the house wall is not plumb, it will be necessary to cut the rafters to different lengths.

GABLE-END ROOF

This type of roof requires both a ridge rafter and common rafters whose ends rest against and are secured to it.

The first step is determining pitch. Doing this mathematically is complicated. It's far easier to simply take it off the plans.

Let us assume for the purposes of this discussion that the pitch is 7½ on 12; that is, the rafters rise 7½

inches for every foot of horizontal distance, which we assume will be 98¼ inches.

The first thing to do is to draw the bird's mouth on the 2 x 6. This notch should be made on a point on the board that will allow for cutting the overhang at the proper point. The board should also be long enough to allow you to cut off the roof end at the proper point.

Referring to Figure 126, use the square to draw the top of the bird's mouth—3½ inches. Draw a plumb line from its end to the edge of the rafter.

Next, mark the rafter (this process is known as "stepping off"); 12 inches of horizontal run into 98½ inches yields eight steps plus 2½ inches. Place the square on the board so the 12-inch mark is aligned with the outside end of the bird's mouth. Inscribe where the 7½-inch mark falls. Then move the square over and set it the same way: a 12-inch mark on the square at the point where the 7½-inch mark was and the 7½-inch mark farther along the edge of the 2 x 6. Move the square along the rafter to make six more markings. When done, the rafter will have eight steps. Draw the last mark all the way across the 2 x 6. To mark the end of the rafter for cutting, measure over 2¼ inches from the last line made with the square and draw a plumb line across the rafter. Mark the lower end of the rafter for cutting, then cut the

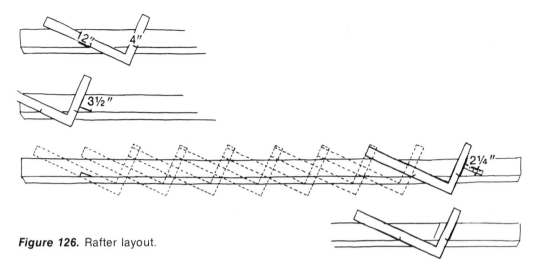

Figure 126. Rafter layout.

rafter—both ends and birds' mouth.

Use this rafter for a pattern and cut another the same way.

Next, test for proper size. Hold the two rafters in position (of course you'll need helpers) with a piece of 2 x 6 (representing the ridge rafter) between them to make sure that you worked it out correctly. If you lay out the rafters before you sheath the walls, you won't have to climb up high to do this; try them right off the deck (bird's mouth can be fitted over shoes). Check that the angle cuts fit at top and bottom, and correct them if necessary. When okay, cut all the rafters.

In some cases, part of a gable roof will intersect with the existing sloping roof.

Cut the end of the ridge rafter (2 x 8) to match the existing roof. If you know the pitch of the house roof,

you can simply mark it off with the framing square. If the pitch of the existing roof is not on the plans, you will have to measure it from the existing roof. Do this with your two-foot level and ruler. Hold the level so it extends directly away from the roof with one end resting on it. When you get a level reading, measure straight down from the outer end of the level to the roof. Do it several times to make sure you did it correctly. Make sure that the ruler is plumb when you read it. Divide this number by 2 to get the pitch in 12 inches or mark it off from the roof, as in Figure 127.

Mark the end of the 2 x 8 with the framing square and make another mark square across the end of the 2 x 8 at the point where this mark reaches the top of the 2 x 8 ridge rafter. Cut on both lines and save the small triangular piece. The 2 x 8 used

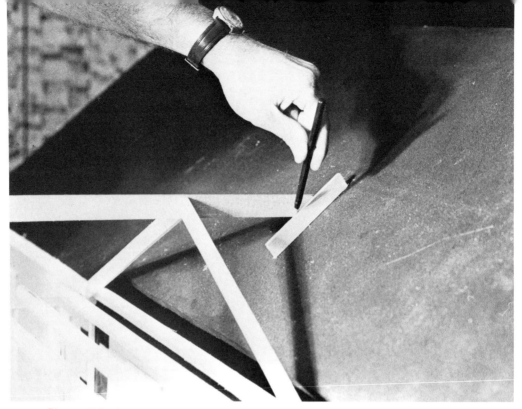

Figure 127. If you don't know the roof pitch, you can mark the pitch of the roof on the rafter by holding a piece of scrap wood against it.

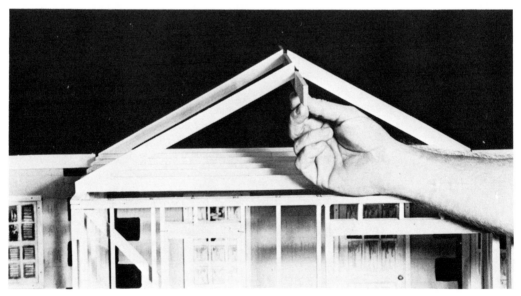

Figure 128. Ridge is forced up between pair of rafters at front and back of extension, and tacked in place.

should be long enough so it extends to well beyond the plate. You'll trim excess as you go.

Lean two pairs of rafters together—one pair at the rear of the extension, one at the front. Nail the rafters to the plate and against the ceiling beams, but leave the tops unnailed. Sight from the outside wall across the tops of the rafters to determine where the ridge rafter will meet the roof. Remove the shingles at this point.

Jockey the ridge rafter under the pair of rafters, and slide its cut end up the roof at the same time, forcing it between the pair of rafters (Fig. 128). Slide the end up the roof and lift the ridge until the end fits tightly

against the roof and the ridge is flush and level at top with the rafter pairs. Loosely nail all the rafters together.

Use a straight stud to plumb down from the ridge to the plate at the outer end (Fig. 129). Mark the end of the ridge and cut it off even with the plate, unless you plan to have the roof overhang.

Starting from the outer end, follow the guide marks on the plate and mark off (on the top edge) the rafter positions along the ridge (Fig. 130). They are on 16-inch centers. Then install the rest of the common rafters. Use the straightest two for the gable ends. Secure the pair closest to the house with their inside edges in line with the facia of the house.

Figure 129. A straight stud is used to plumb down to know where to cut off the end of the rafter.

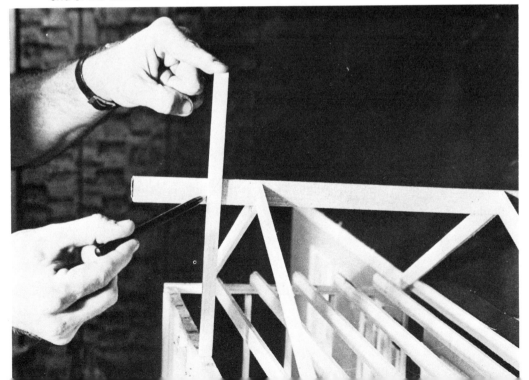

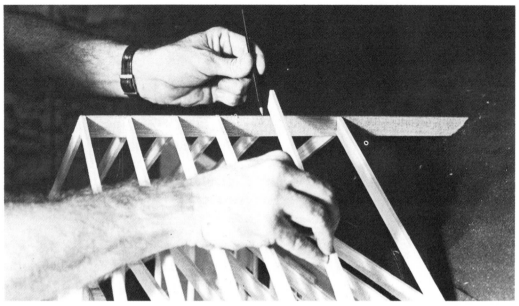

Figure 130. Mark the ridge rafter on top to correspond to marks on the plate, then install common rafters against the ridge rafter.

Figure 131. Chalkline is struck on roof so you'll know where to remove the shingles.

The first pair and last pair will likely be odd distances, but all others will be on 16-inch centers. Pull the nails and move the first two pairs of rafters to their proper marks and, one at a time, nail them in place. You can nail right through the rafter on one side, but the second one of any pair of rafters will have to be toenailed. Use three 10d or 16d common nails to nail through the ridge, or five to toenail.

Valley Rafters

The rafters that extend from the ridge rafters to the roof are the valley rafters.

These rafters can be laid out right on the ground with just a framing square, but it is easier to do it as follows.

First, strike a chalkline on the roof from the end of the ridge where it intersects the house to the lower end of the last common rafters butting the facia (Fig. 131). Remove all whole shingles that this line crosses and clear the roof for at least 1 foot below the line.

The ends of the valley rafters are secured to nailers that are, in turn, secured between the end of the ridge and the end of the common rafter closest to the house. These nailers can be cut from 2 x 6 stock. While neither end has to be a tight fit, both must be located so that their top edges are in the same plane as the top of the common rafters. Indeed,

you want all the rafters in the same plane, so that sheathing can be applied across all without any high or low spots.

To find the proper position, you will need a straight 2 x 4, about 4 or 5 feet long, and a 2 x 6 block. First, lay the 2 x 4 across the rafters at the bottom so it intersects the roof. Slide the block until it fits tightly against the 2 x 4 and the roof. Mark the roof at the edge of the block (Fig. 132).

At the top end, put the block on the roof against the ridge rafter so that its top edge lines up with the top of the ridge (Fig. 133). The best way to do this is to sight along the top of the ridge rafter. Mark the roof at this point, then strike a chalkline across these bottom and top marks.

Nail the 2 x 6 to the roof with its outer edge flush with this line. Mark 16-inch centers on the ridge starting from the last common rafter, then make corresponding marks (for bottom ends of rafters) on the nailer, pulling your tape parallel to the ridge and measuring each one separately 16 inches, 32 inches, 48 inches, etc.

Cutting Valley Rafters

Measure the lengths of valley rafters required from the ridge to the nailer. Measure three consecutive rafter lengths. They will have a common difference.

Cut the top ends at the same angles as the tops of the common rafters. The bottom ends of the rafters are cut at a common angle—

the level cut and at an angle to fit the slope of the roof. To facilitate the latter cut, set your circular saw using the triangular cutoff made when cutting the ridge rafter to fit.

Cut the rafters from stock that is long enough to cut the longest rafter as well as the shortest. Also, cut so the top of the longest rafter is at the end of the 2 x 6. Cut the rafters in order, one pair at a time, doing the longest first. Each pair, of course, should have a common difference in size.

To save on lumber, if you have an odd number of rafters, cut the middle pair from one 2 x 6. After you have cut half the rafters, the others can come out of the off-cuts from the longer rafters. In this way, too, you

should not have to recut the lower ends. Then install the rafters (Fig. 134).

If the gable butts a straight wall, follow the same procedure; the ridge, of course, is already laid out. Remove shingles where the ridge butts the house. Check the outer end for plumb. If it is too long, cut off the house end; if it is too short, shim the house end. You will have to remove the siding from the house where the extension roof butts it.

Put a straight rafter in place at the proper pitch against the house and draw a line on the house that is the length of the rafter. If the siding is asbestos shingles, remove every shingle that this line crosses and any

Figure 132. To establish the line for valley rafters, mark the roof with block, as shown at bottom . . .

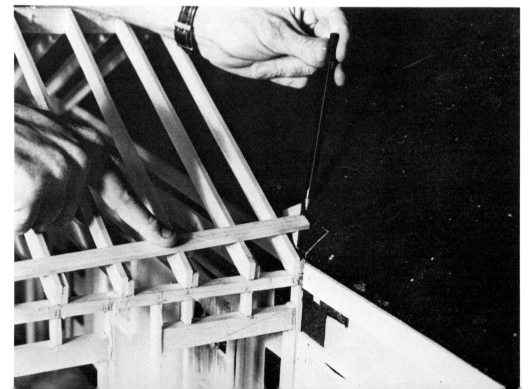

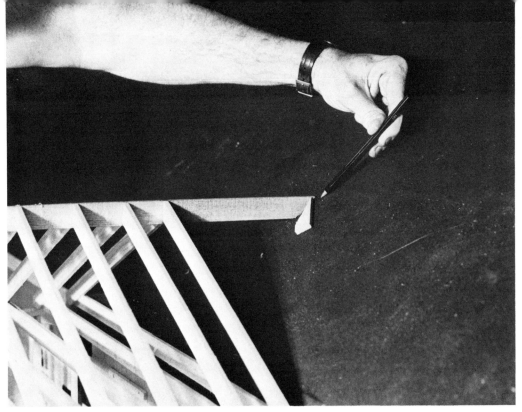

Figure 133. . . . and at top.

Figure 134. With nailer in place, valley rafters are fastened.

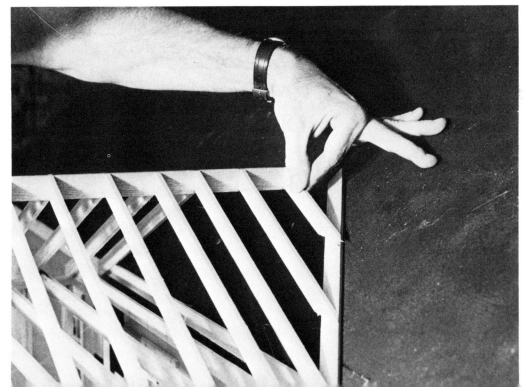

other shingle that the rafter covers. If the siding is wood, strike a line parallel to the first line but 2 inches higher, and cut along it down to the sheathing. Remove the siding below the line to make room for the rafter. Two inches should allow for the thickness of the sheathing and roof shingles and leave a little space between the roofing and the siding. Remove all nails in the siding that are within 5 inches of the top of the rafter.

If you have to butt the brick siding, do nothing now except to secure the rafter to it with lead anchors and screws, installed through the middle.

Gable Studs

The gable studs may be installed next. (You can also install them before the valley rafters, if you wish.)

If you have picked out the straightest rafters for the ends, as mentioned earlier, the studs will have a common difference in length.

Calculate which gable stud will be the longest. Set it on an X mark on the plate. Make it plumb and push it against the rafter. Mark the stud where the rafter crosses, then move the stud to an adjacent X mark and repeat the procedure (Fig. 135). Remove the stud. The distance between the two marks is the common difference between all studs.

Set the circular saw to cut on the angle, then cut the longest stud to length at the angle called for; cut all the other studs, observing the common difference.

Nail the studs in place, plumbing each on its mark as you do. Take care

Figure 135. Measure longest gable stud first.

not to nail them in too tightly or you will bow the rafter in the middle.

Lay out along the plate for the studs from the center. A window should be in the center, flanked by the longest gable stud and jack stud. If there is a louver, use two short studs above the window to flank the louver. If there is just a louver (no window), the studs should flank it (Figs. 136 and 137).

THE HIP ROOF

The first steps in building a hip roof are the same as those for the gable roof, but the ridge rafter is much shorter (Fig. 138). In fact, if the extension is short enough, the end

Figure 136. It is not essential that gable studs be absolutely on their marks, as this illustration shows.

Figure 137. Completed gable end extension.

Figure 138. Ridge rafter on hip roof is much shorter than on gable roof. Note boards on ceiling beams for standing on. They should overlap beams safely.

common rafter and hip rafter will extend over the original roof. Thus, there will not be any common rafters required on the sides; i.e., ones that are secured against the ridge and plate. This situation is unusual and will be covered later.

Usually, you'll have several common rafters on each side. For installing them, you can follow the same procedure as a gable roof, but instead of plumbing down to the plate to find the end of the ridge, hold the end of the common rafter in place and mark the end of the ridge. Cut on this line, nail it in place, then complete all the common rafters and valley rafters as required.

Hip Rafters

Hip rafters also can be laid out with nothing but the framing square, but for just one extension it is easier to do it as follows and as shown in Figures 139 to 144.

1. Cut a block of 2-inch material about 6 inches long and of a width that is the same as the distance from the top of the common rafter to the plate; call this distance *A*.

2. Tack this block diagonally on the corner of the plate, making the end even with the plate corner.

3. Rest the 2 x 8 on this block and the corner formed by the upper ends of the common rafters. The bottom of

the 2 x 8 is now where the top of the rafter should finish up.

4. Draw a plumb line on the 2 x 8 up from the point where it crosses the common intersection, then draw another plumb line up from the outside of the block on the plate. Make a level line for the bird's mouth that is square to this line and the same height above the bird's mouth as the common rafter (distance *A*).

Cut the bird's mouth, then cut the upper end of the 2 x 8 on a 45-degree angle from both sides so it fits into the common-rafter intersection. To do this, use a square to transfer the plumb line on the upper end of the hip rafter to the other side. Cut along both lines at a 45-degree angle (you'll end up with a pointed board).

Put the rafter in place and check the fit. If it fits, nail it in place. You can get the length of the overhang, after the jack rafters (those that go from the hip rafters to the plate) are in place, by holding a straight edge aligned with the cut ends of the jacks and over the hip rafter and marking the length required. Then trim as needed. (See Fig. 144, p. 100.)

Figure 139. To lay out hip rafter, first measure distance shown.

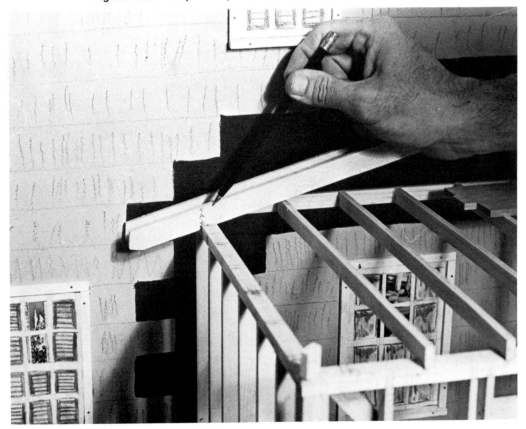

Figure 140. Cut block to size shown and install on corner.

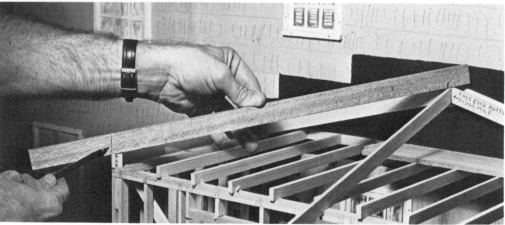

Figure 141. Lay rafter board across as shown and make plumb cuts from the block and where rafters intersect.

Figure 142. Cut both ends of the rafter board and nail in place.

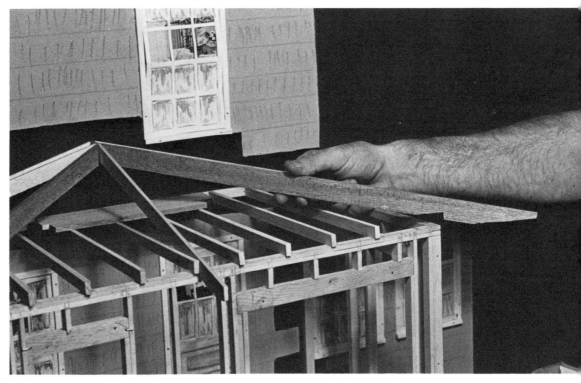

Figure 143. Another view of hip rafter.

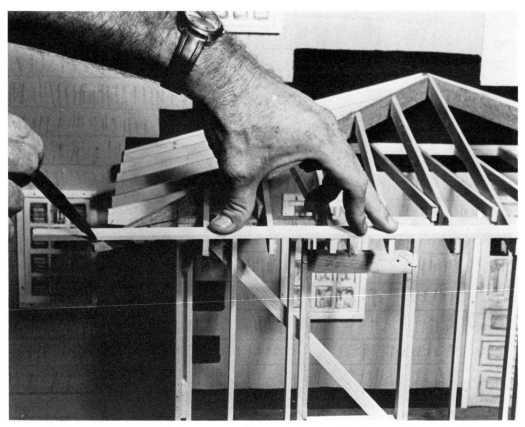

Figure 144. Hold board across rafter, as shown, to know where to trim overhang even with others.

Jack Rafters

Jack rafters are installed next (Figs. 145–152). Like other rafters, they are 16 inches apart. Mark for their upper ends using the common rafter as a guide; that is, mark off 16-inch centers from common rafters. Then extend the tape to adjacent hip rafters and mark off corresponding 16-inch, 32-inch and 48-inch centers.

Measure the distance between the edge of the hip rafter and the plate where the first jack rafter will fall. Measure another, then subtract the numbers (for example, one may be 9 feet 10 inches, the next 9 feet). The result is the common difference between rafter sizes. You can cut all jack rafters on the ground.

The upper end of the jack is the plumb cut—the angle is 45 degrees, the lower end the level (bird's mouth) cut. (The lower end is the same as the common rafter.) Cut the longest and the shortest rafters from the same 2 x 6 (as with valley rafters).

If the overhang is very long, the shortest jack rafter may not reach the plate. If it doesn't make the span between the hip and the next rafter excessively wide (more than 2 feet), it can be omitted.

In some cases on a hip roof you will have only one common rafter abutting the ridge rafter. If so, proceed as follows:

After laying out the common rafter, put a level line on it so that you can check the pitch later. Nail the rafter in place, then cut and fit the ridge from the end of the common rafter to the roof. The top of the ridge must be level. Fasten it in place, then lay out 16-inch centers from the outside end of the ridge. You will have to center it by measuring and brace it temporarily with a 2 x 4 to make sure the common rafter has the proper pitch. Check by holding a level against the level line.

Next, cut the hip rafters as described above and nail them in place. Follow by cutting the jack rafters as above and nail in as many as rest on the plate; cut and fit a pair of jack rafters that are in line with the outside edge of the facia of the existing house.

Follow the procedure described earlier for making the valley rafters; the longest one should fit to the end of the ridge in the same place as a common rafter would. Fill in any remaining gaps with rafters that run from the hip rafter to the valley nailer. These rafters are cut on the top like the jack rafter and on the bottom like a valley rafter. To get the length, lay out their locations exactly and measure them separately. If the old and the new roof have the same pitch, they should all be the same length. (See Fig. 152, p. 106.)

THE FLAT ROOF

While called a flat roof, it actually should pitch about 4 inches for every 10 feet. This type of roof is prone to leaks and should be used only if no other will work. Also, the rafters must be heavier than the rafters in a regular pitched roof of the same size.

As a rule of thumb, the following members should be used:

2 x 8s installed 16 inches o.c. are good for spans up to 12 feet

2 x 10s installed 16 inches o.c. are good for spans up to 14 feet

2 x 12s installed 16 inches o.c. are good for spans up to 16 feet

The angle of the roof is normally so slight that there is no need to make a level cut at the end of the rafters, but the wall ends need a plumb cut so they can fit properly (flush). Some pitch is necessary, though. If you make the roof level and the rafters sag, the roof becomes a large dish and the water will not run off. The slight pitch is just enough to make the water run off.

If the flat roof butts a straight wall, the rafter on the wall end must rest on either a 2 x 4 ledger or nailer secured above the height of the plate to give it the proper pitch.

If the flat roof attaches to another roof, the ends of the rafters must be cut to fit against the existing roof and nailed through the sheathing to the existing rafters. Each new rafter must be directly above an existing rafter.

You can install the rafters over the old shingles. I would prefer to remove them, but then you must finish the new roof right away to keep the rain out.

If you wish to make a level ceiling, install 2 x 6 ceiling beams between the rafters resting on the plate on the outer end and toenailed to the 2 x 4 stringer on the inside end.

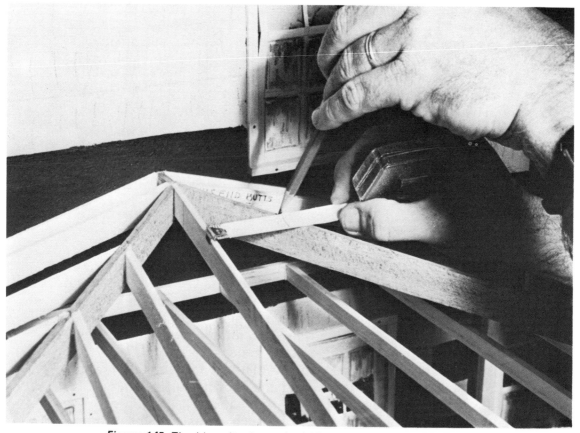

Figure 145. The hip rafter is marked 16 inches from the common rafter . . .

Figure 146. . . . and 32 inches from the common rafter . . .

Figure 147. . . . and 48 inches from the common rafter.

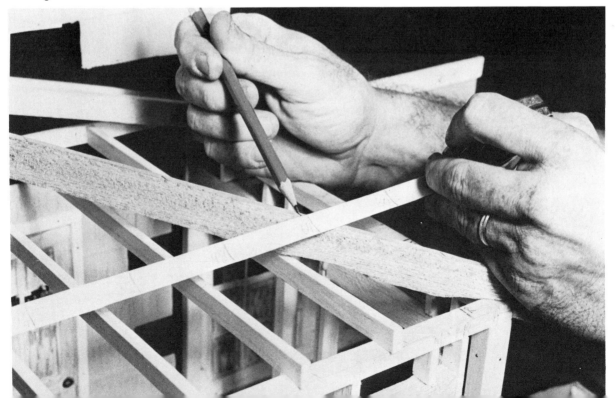

Figure 148. Cut and install the jack rafters in pairs.

Figure 149. Overall view of completed hip roof.

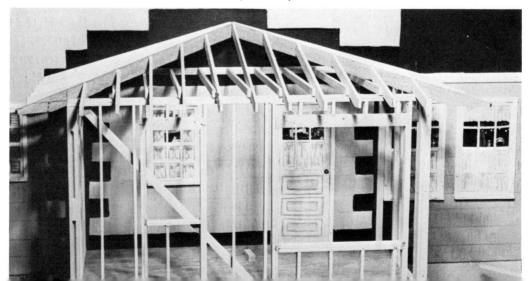

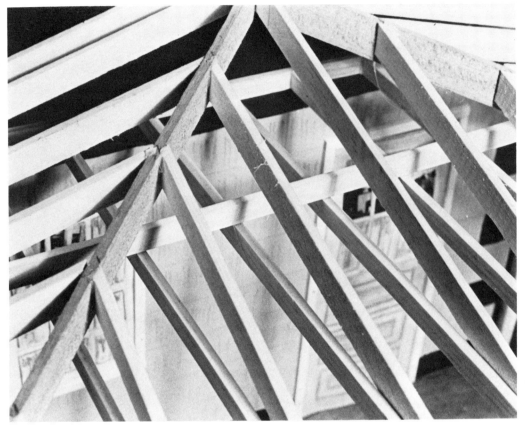

Figure 150. Hip roofs put stress on side walls. Tie walls together with member shown, extending it all the way across walls and nailing it to rafters.

Figure 151. Wall ties should be added to provide nailing surface for Sheetrock.

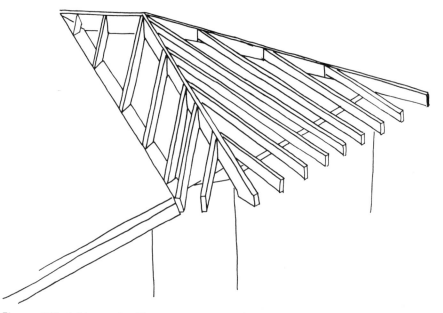

Figure 152. A hip roof with one common rafter in front and none at the sides.

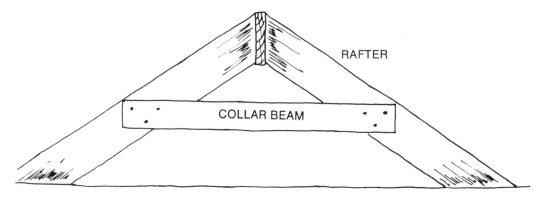

Figure 153. Collar beam.

COLLAR BEAMS

Collar beams are used to tie both sides of a hip and a gable roof together. They may be made from 2 x 4 or 1 x 6 stock and are installed parallel to the joists about one-third the distance down from the top of the ridge to the top of the joists (Fig. 153). Nail one to every third pair of rafters.

ROOF SHEATHING

Once the roof framing is complete, the roof sheathing can be installed (Fig. 154). Although some building codes only require ⅜-inch plywood sheathing, I don't recommend it. If you are going to use plywood, use ½-inch or thicker material.

If you are using plywood sheets, strike chalklines across the rafters 48

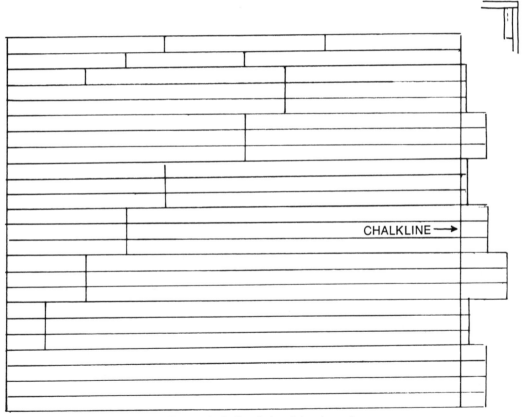

CHALKLINE →

Figure 154. Roof sheathing layout.

inches from their ends. Secure pieces with nails, one nail per rafter. Let pieces overhang the end rafter by ½ inch. To ease the job, cut the plywood on the ground. In this way you won't have to hoist large pieces up to the roof and you don't have to hang off the edge with the circular saw. One by six or 1 x 8 tongue-and-groove or shiplap stock is installed differently. Here, you can nail most of the pieces on without measuring or cutting.

Start with the longest pieces of stock you have, nailing them across the bottom ends of the rafters; if tongue and groove, the tongue should face up; for shiplap, the grooved or rabbet edge is up. Toenail three pieces in place, letting them overlap the edge of the roof, then toenail three more shorter pieces above these. Work your way up the roof. When all are nailed, face-nail them using two nails for 6-inch stock, three for 8-inch. Don't nail hip or end rafters.

Strike a chalkline the thickness of the side-wall sheathing past the rafter ends (or down the middle of a hip rafter), then trim excess with a circular saw. After the sheathing is trimmed, check the end rafter for parallel to the cut, then nail the ends down, straightening the rafter as you do (if required).

Fill in the rest of the roof with pieces that are long enough to overlap the opposite end rafters. Trim as before. Board layout should be planned so that there aren't more than three butts, that is, six pieces butting together, on any one rafter.

CHAPTER 9

Facia and Soffit

The facia is the vertical board on the ends of the rafters or along the gable rake. The soffit is the horizontal board under the rafters, and the frieze is the vertical board or gingerbread on the face of the house adjacent to the soffit (Figs. 155, 156).

The facia is nailed along the rake, or edge, of the roof. Its top edge should be in line with the roof. If you are using asbestos shingles, block out the facia from the edge with a plaster lath to allow room for shingles to be slipped in behind. If you're installing cedar shingles, use 1 x 4; use 2 x 4 for hand-split shakes.

Before installing the facias, cut a length of 15-pound felt 18 inches wide and as long as the rake. Staple it over the edge of the roof—half on top and half on the edge. Nail on the spacing material with 4d nails for lath or 8d nails for 1 x 4; use 10d nails for 2 x 4. Nail the facias on with 8d common nails and set their heads below the surface.

The frieze can be added as needed, according to how the rafters are framed. A variety of possibilities is shown in Figure 157. (See also Figs. 158–160.)

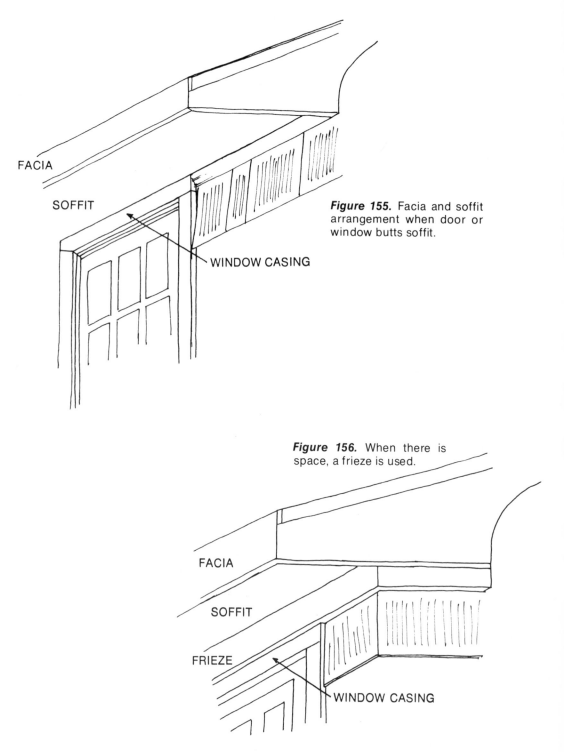

FACIA

SOFFIT

Figure 155. Facia and soffit arrangement when door or window butts soffit.

WINDOW CASING

Figure 156. When there is space, a frieze is used.

FACIA

SOFFIT

FRIEZE

WINDOW CASING

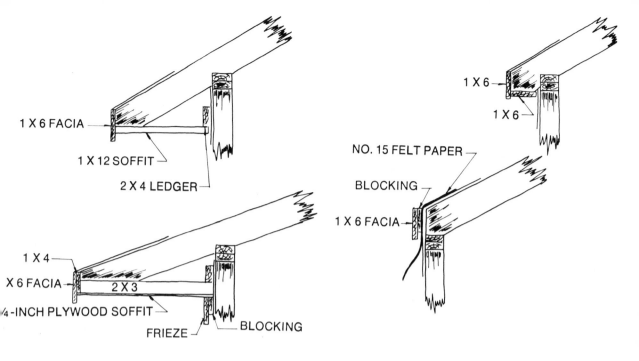

1 X 6 FACIA

1 X 12 SOFFIT

2 X 4 LEDGER

1 X 6

1 X 6

NO. 15 FELT PAPER

BLOCKING

1 X 6 FACIA

1 X 4

X 6 FACIA

2 X 3

¼-INCH PLYWOOD SOFFIT

FRIEZE

BLOCKING

Figure 157. Various ways one can trim out the ends of rafters.

Figure 158. Soffit in place. Mark end of facia with level to make sure it's plumb.

Figure 159. Cut off the end piece even with soffit.

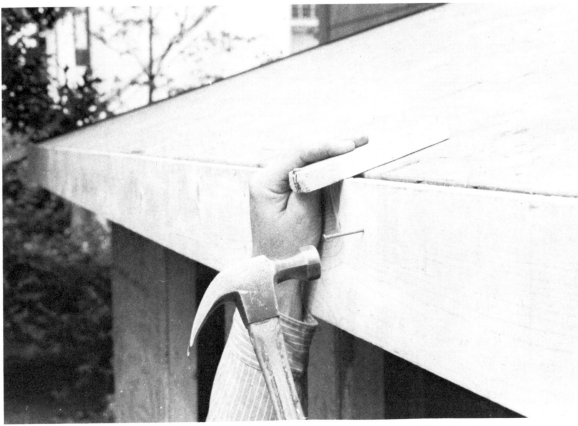

Figure 160. A block of wood is used to align facia when nailing in place.

CHAPTER **10**

Installing Roof Shingles

There are a variety of materials one may install on the roof but the most common are asphalt shingles (Fig. 161). Following are tips on how to install them on a shed-type roof that you can adapt for other types of roofs.

Applying asphalt shingles requires two materials: the shingles and 15-pound felt for watertightness beneath them. For safety it is best to install a few courses of shingles to stand on before doing the rest of the job. Felt alone is too slippery to be safe.

INSTALLING FELT

First, unroll a piece of felt (also called tarpaper) along the left edge (as you face it) of the roof, and trim it flush with a utility knife (Figs. 162, 163). Secure the piece with large-head roofing nails or staples. (Fig. 164). Unroll another piece of felt along the bottom of the roof; this one should overlap the first about 3 inches. Cut it flush as needed with the roof edges.

After the first two pieces of tarpaper are installed, snap chalklines along the left edge of the roof, one 5¼ inches away and the other 11¼ inches (Fig. 165). These lines will serve as vertical guides so that you can place full and parts of shingles to overlap the roof edge by ¾ inch. (The layout is such that there won't be any gaps for water leaks—the roof will be covered by a uniform mass of shingles.)

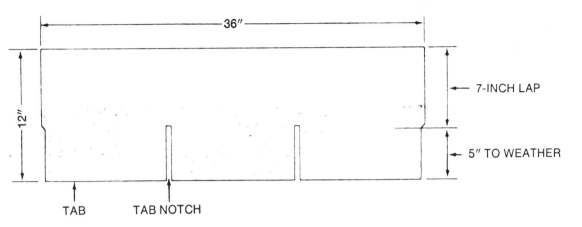

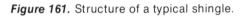

Figure 161. Structure of a typical shingle.

Figure 162. Unroll pieces of felt (also known as tarpaper), one along left edge of roof and one along the bottom edge. Pieces should overlap a few inches.

Figure 163. Trim pieces of felt or tarpaper with utility knife.

Figure 164. Staple felt pieces on or use roofing nails.

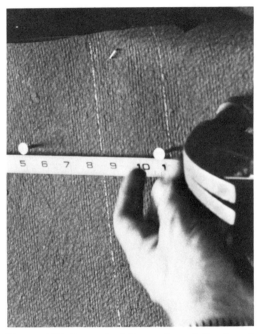

Figure 165. Snap chalklines along left edge of roof, one 5¼ inches from roof edge, the other 11¼ inches. Nails are handy for anchoring chalkline.

As a guide to horizontal placement, drive a nail in on each side of the roof 10 inches from the bottom edge, then drive additional nails all the way up the edges, also 10 inches apart (Fig. 166). Snap a chalkline between the first two nails. Using this as a guide, install a starter course of shingles; that is, side-by-side shingles upside down along the bottom edge of the roof (Fig. 167). Secure with large-head roofing nails (as shown in Figure 173). So placed, they will overlap the bottom edge of the roof 2 inches, because shingles are 12 inches deep.

Follow the details in Figures 168 to 182 for placing shingles on top of the starter course and for subsequent courses. The first course should align with the starter course; subsequent courses overlap the one below it and align at the top with chalklines extending between nails. The second course should overlap the first, and the bottom of the second course should be aligned with the top of the vents in the course below it. Alternate courses should be aligned with the chalklines. (After four or five courses have been installed, you can nail roof brackets to the roof to hold boards that will serve as scaffolding.) As the illustrations show, it will be necessary to cut some shingles to accomplish this. When shingles need to be cut, score them deeply on the back, and bend them to break.

Shingles on the right side of the roof are cut so they overhang ¾ inch. To ensure this, nail a 1 x 2 flush with the top of the roof. It is ¾ inch thick. When a shingle overlaps, simply nick it with your utility knife at top and bottom where it intersects with the 1 x 2, then trim off excess, scoring the shingle deeply in the back.

In some cases, shingle layout will result in the last tab on the shingle being very narrow—1½ inches or less—and a good stiff wind can blow these small pieces off the roof. To avoid this, follow this procedure: cut away the small section and a whole tab adjacent to it. Trim alternate courses back.

Figure 166. For horizontal guidelines, drive nails up edge of roof 10 inches apart; snap chalklines off them.

Figure 167. A starter course of shingles. Vents (slots) are upside down; course overlaps roof ¾ inch at the side and 2 inches at the bottom.

Figure 168. Cut shingles from back, using square.

Figure 169. The second shingle is cut in the center of the vent.

Figure 170. Layout of shingles: First (from bottom left) is two and a half tabs wide, second is two tabs, then one and a half tabs, and so on. Each is 6 inches less than the one before it.

Figure 171. To cut shingle, score it across the back.

Figure 172. After scoring shingle, fold it up to break it cleanly.

Figure 173. Regular shingles installed over starter course. Note that vents are facing down with the nails placed to sides of vent, not directly above.

Figure 174. First complete set of shingles installed.

Figure 175. View of the other end of roof.

Figure 176. Second "pyramid" of shingles in place.

Figure 177. When cutting shingles for the edge, tack a ¾-inch board there, place shingle, and nick it at top and bottom where it intersects board.

Figure 178. Use square to cut piece of shingle.

Figure 179. Nail shingle piece so its edge is aligned with board edge. When you remove the board, you'll have a neat ¾-inch overlap.

Figure 180. Top of shingles may have to be trimmed in order to have proper overlap of shingles below.

Figure 181. Nailing last shingles in place.

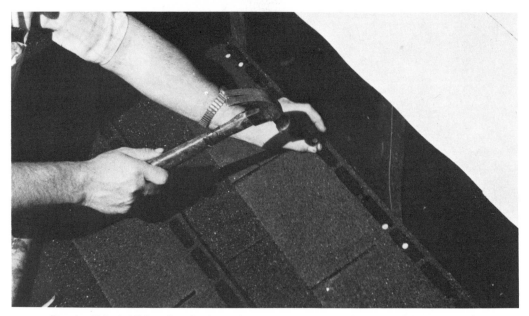

Figure 182. Additional nails have been pounded in. When all shingles are in place, apply black caulk between roof and house wall for sealing under flashing.

Cut another shingle section the same width but with the end tab 3 inches; if the end tab works out to be 1 inch wide, the total width of it and the tab next to it is 13 inches. You should, therefore, cut the piece with a 10-inch tab on the left side and a 3-inch tab on the right. Use this as a template for cutting pieces for alternate courses.

FLASHING

Flashing is the material used to seal the gaps between roofing and walls and between sections of roofing in a valley. It is a thin aluminum that comes in 50-foot rolls and in various widths—commonly, 6 feet, 8 feet, 10 feet, 12 feet, and 14 feet. It is available at building supply stores. Different applications require that it be bent to different shapes. Some dealers will do this for you, usually in lengths up to 8 feet; it is suggested that you buy from one of these dealers. If pieces longer than 8 feet are required (and they likely will be), then you can overlap sections.

The sketches—Figs. 183, 184, 185, and 186—indicate various types.

Apron flashing should be 8 inches wide, bent in the middle with 4 inches overlapping the roof and the other 4 inches up against the wall. Nail the flashing with roofing nails into the wall.

Valley flashing is used between roofing sections in a roof valley. This should be 12 inches wide, creased in the center, and have rolled-over edges. Lay it on a strip of felt slightly wider than the flashing, with the edges, as indicated, under the old and new roofing. Secure it with nails through the top end only (½ inch from the end); these top nails should be covered with another section of flashing or the cap shingles. Also secure the rolled edges by driving roofing nails next to them so the edges of the nail heads hold the flashing edges down but do not penetrate or flatten them. You don't want water leaking in around the nails or edges.

Rake flashing is used where the roof joins the side of the extension wall. It is a cross between apron and valley flashing—nailed to the wall. Again, take care not to flatten the rolled edges; this could cause a leak.

Step flashing can be used instead of rake flashing. It can be bought in 5" x 7" pieces. To use the pieces, first bend them in half lengthwise. Nail one piece under the lower edge of each shingle that abuts the side wall.

One final note on using flashing: Water running down flashing must either be run directly off the roof, or on top of the shingles to drip off below. Never give water a chance to get under the shingles.

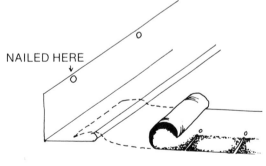

NAIL HERE

4″

Figure 183. Apron flashing.

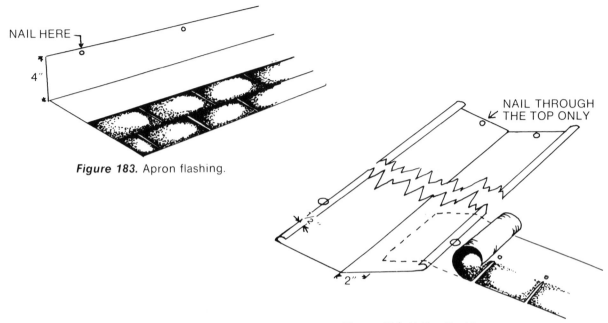

NAIL THROUGH THE TOP ONLY

½″

2″

Figure 184. Valley flashing.

NAILED HERE

Figure 185. Rake flashing.

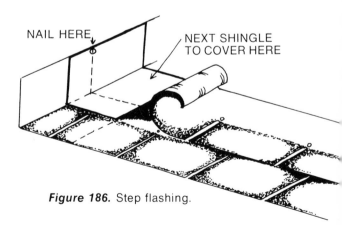

NAIL HERE

NEXT SHINGLE TO COVER HERE

Figure 186. Step flashing.

CHAPTER **11**

Installing Windows and Doors

WINDOWS

When shopping for windows, it is necessary that you select those of high quality. Windows can be very important in terms of energy saving and in terms of causing the least amount of aggravation.

There are many types of windows available. The top-of-the-line are vinyl-clad windows (such as Andersen makes) featuring insulated glass—a sandwich of glass with a dead-air space between. The vinyl can be wiped clean with a rag and the windows won't require painting. This type of window eliminates the need for storm windows.

Lower in quality—but still good —are single-glazed windows with metal weather-stripping. These do a very good job of keeping drafts out. However, wood windows are especially recommended. They won't warp like metal windows and they have a greater capacity to seal.

The rough opening for standard double-hung windows is made 2 inches wider than their nominal width. For specialty windows these figures are listed in the lumberyard's catalog. Make a note of them when you order your windows.

"Before" and "After" Sheathing Windows

In general, there are two types of windows: those designed to be installed before the sheathing is in and those designed for installation after the sheathing is in. The easiest type of installation for an addition is an after-sheathing window.

Installation

A window may be picked up at a local lumberyard or delivered. If you pick it up yourself, carry it so that the putty side is up. In this way the glass won't bear down on the glazier's points—the devices that hold the glass in place.

Remove the protective horns, then slip the window into the opening from the outside (Fig. 187). Move it until there is about a ¼-inch space on each side, or at least equal space. Set a level on the back of the sill, which slopes, making sure the tool is parallel with the bottom of the window.

The window will probably be a bit unlevel. So, determine the high side and drive a 10d nail through the casing and sheathing into a jack stud about 5 inches up from the sill. Leave the head out so you can pull the nail if required.

Use the level to check the window for plumb on the same side (Fig. 188). If it is plumb, drive a 10d nail through casing sheathing and into the jack stud. Also leave the head exposed. If it isn't plumb, have a helper use a pry bar on the inside to get it that way, then drive your nail in 4 to 5 inches from the top.

Place the level on the back edge of the sill again. Pry the window up with a bar. When it's level, drive a nail through the casing into the jack stud 5 inches or so from the sill on the opposite side. Check for plumb and level. If the window is plumb, drive the nails home and set them. If it is not, remove the nails and start over.

When the window is plumb and level, drive additional nails through the casing and into the jack studs spaced about a foot apart (Fig. 189). If the window is less than 2 feet wide, don't use any nails on the top. If 3 to 4 feet wide, use one nail centered in the window. Use two nails for widths greater than 5 feet.

Before you drive those other nails home, however, you should check the window for easy operation. In some cases you'll have to leave the window a bit out-of-square to make it work properly. With good-quality windows, however, this usually isn't required.

Exterior door jambs are installed in the same manner, except you will have to use a straightedge to check the sides for straightness before you nail it home.

DOORS

Installing a door in an existing opening is a job that can challenge the skill of even the most experienced carpenters. However, installing one in an addition is not nearly so problematic, as long as you were careful to get the door framing plumb and level as you constructed the addition.

Figure 187. The first step in installing a window is to cut off protective horns.

Figure 188. The window is slipped into place. (Strips of tarpaper will serve to make the edges of the window watertight.) Check for plumb and level.

Figure 189. When window is plumb and level, nail securely.

Kinds of Doors

There are two kinds of doors: interior and exterior. Also, doors may be flush—have a flat surface—or be of the sash type, that is, constructed of various parts, like a window.

Interior and exterior doors differ in the kind of glue used to construct them. On exterior doors, quite simply, the glue is designed to withstand weather. Usually, exterior doors are thicker than the interior type. The thicker the door, the better it can stand up to weather.

A flush interior door may be made of solid wood or be hollow—an outside covering of veneer, with an inside filling, such as cardboard. Exterior flush doors may be hollow or solid. The core of a solid exterior door should be all wood (no fiber filler).

The run-of-the-mill veneer on doors will be luan, which is really just meant to be painted, but better doors can be ordered with birch, oak, or other hardwood veneers.

The sash door, as mentioned, is

composed of parts, like a window. It also comes in the same thickness as flush doors. You'll find sash doors, which all come unfinished, available in a greater variety of styles than flush doors; both types of doors (flush and sash) are available with glass. Take care to select a door that matches the style of your house and addition.

Installation

As mentioned earlier, if the door framing is correct, installation will not pose any problem (Figs. 190–192).

1. Choose a door of the correct nominal size.

2. Cut (use a circular saw) the door to correct height, which is ½ inch or more (allowing clearance for rugs) shorter than the jamb height. You must plane half of the excess width off each side of the door to end up ⅛ inch narrower than jamb width.

3. Bevel the latch edge of the door to allow clearance for the door to swing.

4. Install hinges. Use a butt gauge to mark out the hinges and chisel out the mortises. The top of the upper hinge should be 5 to 6 inches lower than the top of the door. The top of the lower hinges should be about 12 inches off the floor. Exterior doors should have a third hinge centered between these two hinges.

5. Hang the door on the hinges. There should be $1/16$-inch clearance at both sides and the top.

6. Try the door to make sure that it swings without scraping the jamb and that there is enough clearance at the hinge side. If not, take it down and plane it off where it touches.

Figure 190. Door installation procedures are basically the same as window installation procedures.

Figure 191. After plumbing, check to see if the door jamb is level.

Figure 192. Installing the interior door jamb.

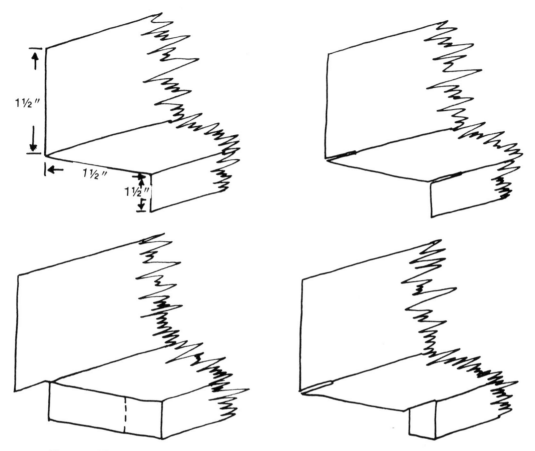

Figure 193. A drip cap should be installed over all doors and windows. In sequence (clockwise, from top left), the ends of the cap are cut with snips, then the pieces are bent over to close ends. The drip cap is nailed through the back flange for attaching.

DRIP CAP

The tops of all windows and door frames must be covered with a drip cap, except when the window casing is butted to the soffit or facia board. The drip cap is bent aluminum or copper stock. Nail it through the back flange only; the horizontal por- tion should pitch slightly from back to front. The back flange should be tight to the wall, directly against the sheathing, and have 15-pound felt laid over it. The ends of the drip cap are cut and bent over the ends of the window casing, as shown in Figure 193.

CHAPTER **12**

Siding

KINDS OF SIDING

There are many kinds of siding one can use on an extension. Following is a summary:

• Plywood siding comes in a variety of styles and in pieces 8 feet long. Installation is similar to installing prefinished paneling. It is applied vertically with half-lap edges butted on the studs.

• Clapboard siding is called "beveled siding" in the lumberyard. It is usually made of redwood or pine and comes in various widths, but it is really "one by" material resawn diagonally.

Clapboard siding is installed with 4d galvanized nails; one nail is driven into each stud 1 inch from the bottom of the board. Installation should start from the bottom board and work up. Lattice is installed under the first course to block it out and give it a raised look like other pieces.

Corners on clapboard siding may be handled a couple of ways. In one instance, $5/4$ by 2-inch pine or redwood may be nailed at right angles with a piece of ¾-inch half-round between. Another way is to install the pieces so that they butt and overlap one another.

Clapboard—in fact any siding—is installed with part of it exposed to the weather: the part not covered by the course(s) above. For example, 1 x 6 should be 4 inches to the weather.

It is best, when installing this type of siding, to draw chalkline guides on the wall to ensure straightness; it is highly likely that the siding will not be completely straight. Corners under the soffit can be covered with molding; the top of the siding should be slipped under the facia.

• Cedar shingles are quite common. Also called shakes, they are made in several grades and varieties and are applied in several different ways.

• Regular sawn shingles come in random widths and are 18 or 24 inches high and ⅜ or ½ inch thick at the butt, or bottom. They are parallel on the sides, and the butt ends are more or less square (grades are perfections No. 1 or No. 2 and undercourse). Machine-grooved or striated shingles are the same but are only made in 18-inch lengths. The face side is striated or grooved.

• Hand-split shakes are another kind. These shingles are not parallel-sided or square. The butts range from ⅜ to 1¼ inches thick. They are sorted into three groups by thickness: ⅜ to about ½ inch, ½ to ¾ inch, and ¾ to 1¼ inches. The thinner ones are somewhat less expensive. The actual range in thickness can be ⅜ to ¾ inch, ½ to 1 inch, and ¾ to 2 inches. They are available in 18-inch or 24-inch lengths.

Cedar shingles may be installed with or without undercourse shingles. An undercourse pushes the bottom of the shingles out and produces a shadow effect.

When shingles are applied without an undercourse, they must have at least a 2-inch "head lap," which is the part of the shingle covered by both of the next two courses. This is to prevent leakage.

An 18-inch shingle should not be applied more than 8 inches to the weather; a 24-inch shingle should not be more than 11 inches. Eighteen-inch striated shingles are commonly applied with an undercourse about 14 inches to the weather.

In general, it is a sign of a good job when the bottoms of the shingle courses are even with the tops and bottoms of windows. It is not always possible to do this with all window bottoms, but you can make the shingles even with the tops and the bottoms of the windows that are the most common size.

INSTALLING SHINGLES

In installing shingles, the first step is to apply 15-pound felt to the sheathing, stapling it on, or securing it with roofing nails (Fig. 194). To do this, cut off a piece from the roll as long as the area to be covered. Reroll it, then roll it out on the sheathing with one edge aligned with the bottom of the sheathing. Tack the felt as you unroll it, just enough to make it stay in place and lie flat against the wall.

After the first strip is in place, you

Figure 194. Felt or tarpaper is applied across sheathing and stapled in place as a base for shingles.

are ready to apply the shingles. Additional pieces of felt should be added as you go, with pieces overlapping 3 inches. Regardless of the kind of shingles you are using, the first course is installed the same way. It should extend 1 inch below the sheathing. To ensure straightness, it's best to use a guide. For the guide, choose a straight 2 x 4, 10 or 12 feet long. Nail it to a board, such as plaster lath, which in turn is nailed to the sheathing so the 2 x 4 hangs level 1 inch below the bottom of the sheathing. Nail additional plaster lath to the bottom of the sheathing so the shingles of the first course will be angled the same as the courses above (Figs. 195–196).

There are some variations when installing different types of shingles. On regular sawn shingles, the first course (there is no need for an undercourse) should be double, and joints should be staggered at least 1 inch. (The latter is true for all kinds of shingles.)

To begin, rest the butt ends of the first layer of shingles on the 2 x 4 guide, securing each with a nail or staple. Leave ⅛ inch of space between shingles. Install the second layer in the same way, nailing each on with two 4d galvanized common nails; nails should be 1 inch from the edge and 1 inch above the bottom of the next course.

Subsequent courses should be spaced so they are even distances apart, but not more than 8 inches to the weather if 18-inch shingles, or 11 inches if 24-inch shingles, as mentioned earlier. To do this, divide the distance from the bottom of the first

Figure 195. Lath is installed on tarpaper.

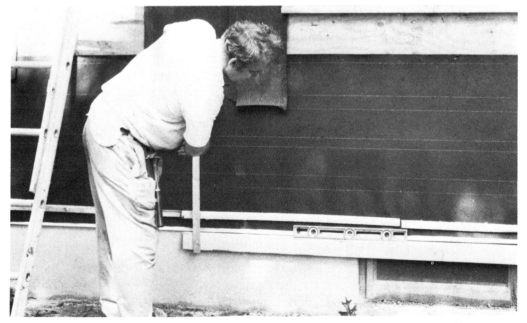

Figure 196. A 2 x 4 guide is then secured to lath 1 inch below sheathing. Note level on guide.

Figure 197. Several striated shingle courses in place. Note guide beneath one course and guide (wider board) nailed in place for course above.

course to the bottom of the window-sill and the height of the window into approximately even spaces. For example, if the window height were 55 inches and the shingles were 24 inches, dividing 55 by 11 (11 inches to weather) equals five courses of shingles 11 inches to the weather. That would work. If distance below the window were 41¼ inches, you can divide 4 into it and get 10¼ inches of space to the weather. The important point is to get shingles that are approximately the same height to the weather for a uniform appearance. To place these courses level, strike chalklines for them and use a piece of 1 x 2 tacked to the chalkline as a guide (Fig. 197).

Again, if your windows are of different heights, make the courses work out even with the most common size. Figure the greatest width of windows, not the greatest number of windows.

CORNERS

Corners on striated and regular cedar shingles can be handled in two ways. One way is with wood trim.

The second method, while more difficult, looks better but is not as

Figure 198. A piece of undercourse for striated shingles being applied so it is flush with edge of house (regular shingles are handled the same way at corners).

easy to do nor will it stand up as well in a vulnerable spot, such as near a walkway. Here, no trim is used; shingles are cut to overlap. Start with the bottom course. Hold the shingle so that it rests on the 2 x 4 guide and extends past the end of the house about ½ to 1 inch. Mark where the lath falls on the back of the shingle, and also where the top of the shingle meets the corner of the house.

Remove the shingle and connect the two marks with a straight line. Trim the shingle to this line. You can do this with a straightedge and a utility knife; or, use a sharp hatchet to cut away most of the waste, then finish with a block plane.

Check the shingle to make sure it fits properly against the corner. If it is too big, plane it down to fit. If too small, move it over until the edge aligns properly. The mate to this shingle on the adjacent side can be placed using a level to keep it plumb.

Do the second course the same way, but install the side shingle first and the front shingle over its end. Keep the edges of the shingles 1 inch or more away from the edge of the shingle in the course below.

The third course is lapped in the same direction as the first. Lap each succeeding course opposite to the one below.

The top of the last course may be butted to the soffit and covered with

Figure 199. Shingle on adjacent corner overlaps it.

Figure 200. Undercourse in place. Note that the undercourse doesn't have to butt guide strip perfectly.

Figure 201. Face shingle is placed on corner and made plumb.

Figure 202. Back of shingle is marked for cutting.

Figure 203. Marking other half of shingle.

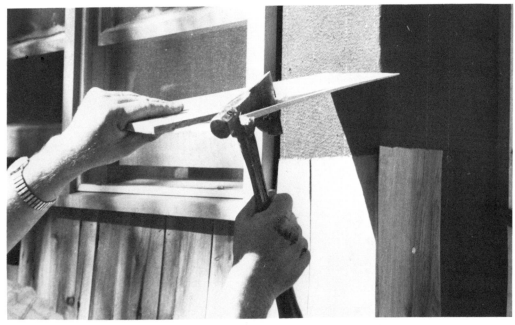

Figure 204. Shingles can be trimmed with a hatchet . . .

Figure 205. . . . and finished with a block plane.

Figure 206. Nailing shingle in place. Note that bottom edge aligns with guide.

Figure 207. Alternate courses overlap in opposite ways. Note that shingle is even with bottom of window.

Figure 208. Shingles under window should recess into slot on sill.

a bed molding or the end tucked under the facia. Nail the last course on with 6d galvanized finishing nails.

STRIATED SHINGLES

Striated shingles are installed like sawn ones except you use an undercourse, held up from the guides and the finish courses butted together. The undercourse can be stapled on and need not be fitted together; ¼- to ½-inch spaces are acceptable. Or, use backer board for an undercourse. These are 16″ x 48″ x ¼″ sections of fiberboard made for this purpose. Face-nail the shingles with 6d finishing nails driven 2 inches above the butt and 2 inches apart (Fig. 209). This will keep the shingles from buckling—spaces are left in the sawn shingles to allow room for expansion (Fig. 210).

Courses are installed the same way as for sawn shingles. To achieve a dental effect on any shingle with square butts, you can use a ½-inch block of wood as a spacer between the guide and every other shingle.

Corners of regular sawn and striated shingles are handled in the same way (Figs. 198–208).

HAND-SPLIT SHINGLES

Hand splits can be laid using either of the methods described, but use 6d common nails or 8d finishing nails. Use the 2 x 4 guide for the first course. Strike a chalkline for succeeding courses, but do not use the 1 x 2. Just cover the line with the butt of the shingles. Butts are not square and this will give a random look while keeping the courses even.

ASBESTOS SHINGLES

Asbestos shingles come in a variety of colors and are quite popular. While inexpensive, they are brittle and can be broken fairly easily. Like other shingles, they are installed over 15-pound felt, one piece at a time.

First strike a chalkline on the felt to align the top of the first course. While shingles come with holes, you will have to make extra holes for the first course because the factory-made ones are 1 inch from the edge and the shingle should overhang the sheathing by 1 inch. Use a shingle cutter (which you can rent) to make these holes, locating them 1 inch above the existing ones (Fig. 211).

Next, install the corner molding. Corners can be handled in one of three ways:

• Continuous aluminum corners. Nail these over the felt with roofing nails, making sure they are tight to the corner and straight. The corners are made in two ways. The first way, as shown in Figure 212 (top) is the original method not much used anymore. This made a quarter-round effect but the shingles had to fit tightly to it. Later, the second molding came

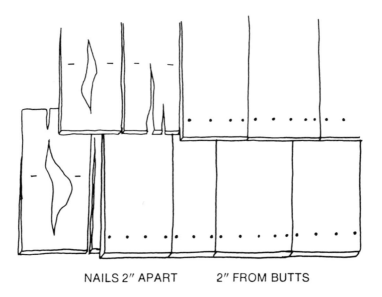

NAILS 2″ APART   2″ FROM BUTTS

Figure 209. Nailing schedule for striated shingles.

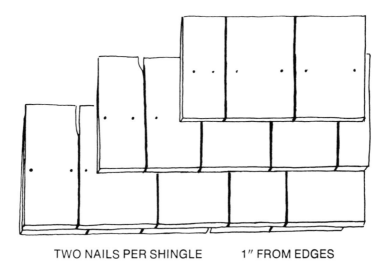

TWO NAILS PER SHINGLE   1″ FROM EDGES

Figure 210. Nailing schedule for regular sawn shingles.

into use. With this, shingles fit into a groove; since a perfect fit is not required, the overall look is generally better (Fig. 212 [middle]).

• Individual corners for each course. These corners slip over the ends of each course and are nailed above the course.

• Wooden corners. This involves securing a piece of 1 x 4 along the edge of the wall and is useful when you have different kinds of siding on adjacent sides of the corner. Let the 1 x 4 extend beyond the corner far enough so that adjacent siding can butt it (Fig. 212 [bottom]).

Start installation in a corner. Hold the top of a corner shingle on the chalkline and drive three nails through the holes. Don't drive the

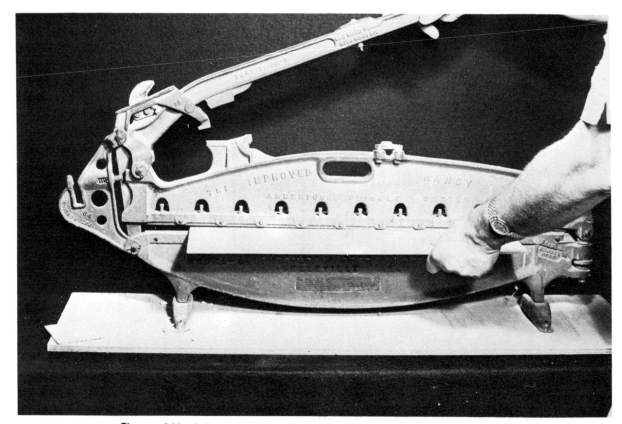

Figure 211. Asbestos shingle cutter. Note projection near end of handle and one near front (hooked, facing front) for punching holes in shingles. Equipment rental dealer will tell you how to use it.

end nail home until you have slipped the felt tab (these come with the shingles and seal joints) under the shingle. Continue to install other shingles in the course. Each should butt tightly to ones adjacent and be aligned on the chalkline. However, if placement dictates a choice between proper butting or alignment, choose alignment; otherwise, the rest of the shingles will be crooked.

The joints of the second course are staggered by starting with a half shingle above a full shingle. Put a nail through the hole in the shingle rest the nail on top of the shingle below, and drive the nail. Do the same with the other two nails, making sure the nails go in horizontally. If you pitch the nails up or down, the shingles will be out of line.

Asbestos shingles must be installed without regard to how the courses work out by windows and doors. If you wind up with a very narrow course under a window, you'll just have to live with it. After the shingles are installed, they should be caulked wherever the ends of the shingles butt wood, such as between shingles and windows. The tops of the shingles should be fitted under the facia or butted against the soffit, and then covered by a bed molding.

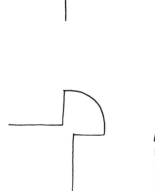

Figure 212. Corner treatments. Top: asbestos shingles slide into recess so careful fitting isn't required. Middle: careful fitting is required. Bottom: wood corner for asbestos and cedar shingles.

ASBESTOS
SHINGLES
BUTT HERE

1 X 4

CEDAR SHINGLES
BUTT HERE

CHAPTER **13**

Tips on Doing Electrical Work

Before you do any electrical work, you should determine just what is and is not permitted by your local building code. And, after the work is finished, be sure to have it inspected by a licensed electrical contractor and/or get an underwriter's certificate. If you don't and a fire occurs because of your work, then your fire insurance may be declared invalid.

If allowed, you should use No. 12 wire for outlets, assuming you are just going to be using lamps or small appliances in the extension. While you may not need wire that is this heavy now, it gives you easy future capacity for adding more switches and receptacles without great difficulty. No. 14 wire is sufficient for lights and switches.

If your code allows it, use Romex wire. It is more flexible and easier to use than the other common type, BX. Make sure that the wire has a ground and ensure that it is used.

You should plan the electrical circuits so that they take the most direct route from the fuse box or circuit-breaker panel to the particular electrical facility. In this way you will have a minimum amount of drilling of framing members to do.

If possible, plan so you avoid cutting framing when running wire to the addition. A handy place, usually, to run a wire is along a sill plate in a basement, where it can be secured with staples. Holes are then drilled through the framing members into the addition. If you must drill holes in structural members such as joists and studs, the holes should be drilled in the middle of the members, i.e., the middle of their widths.

Boxes for housing the switches and receptacles are commonly available at electrical-supply stores. They are simple to install—just nail their flanges to framing members. Some codes specify plastic boxes while others specify metal.

GROUNDED DEVICES

For safety, it is a good idea to use only those devices that can be grounded. Also, consider installing ground fault circuit interrupters (GFI's). Indeed, some codes require GFI's wherever there is going to be water, such as in the kitchen or bath. There are a few types of these available, but all basically function by being able to detect minute leakages of electricity, which can build up enough to overload a circuit or deliver a shock. Of the two common types used in the home, most people prefer the receptacle kind; it is simply a receptacle that's also a GFI. The other kind, installed at the electrical panel in place of a circuit breaker, can be a nuisance. It does its job so well that it can have you running all day to the electrical panel to reactivate a circuit tripped or fuse blown by a minute leakage.

FIXTURES

Hardware for mounting ceiling and wall fixtures greatly simplifies fixture installation. On one type, boxes come with flanges or bars that attach to exposed framing members.

SAVING MONEY

Electrical work is mostly hard labor rather than sophisticated handiwork. As such, if you nail on all the boxes, drill all the holes, pull all the wire through, and staple the wire as necessary, you will have done the major portion of it—and have saved money. Your electrician can lay it out for you before you start and make the final hookup to the electrical panel.

To save time and effort, make all wall outlet boxes exactly the same height off the floor; 15 inches is a good height. To facilitate this, cut a guide stick from a 1 x 2, 15 inches long, and use it to place each box. Knowing the height will enable you to know where to cut the Sheetrock and paneling when you are installing them. And if you should accidentally cover a box, you will know how high to cut for it.

Make all switches 48 inches high to the center. This will place them right in the seam in the horizontally installed Sheetrock and will enable you to see them. With all the boxes in place, you can more easily see where you will have to drill holes in the framing for the wire. For speed, you should drill all the holes before you start to run the wire, and run the entire wire for each circuit before you start another.

One other tip: All outlets and lights in one room should not be on the same circuit; if so, and you find yourself working on the lighting at night, you will have to work in the dark!

CHAPTER **14**

Insulation

As you undoubtedly know, it makes a lot of sense today to install insulation. When you add a room, the job is greatly simplified because the studs and ceiling beams are exposed and the type of insulation used—batts or blankets—are quite simple to install on framing members.

Batts and blankets are simply strips of insulation. They may be mineral wool, rock wool, or fiberglass, but all come just wide enough to fit between framing members that are spaced a standard 16 inches apart. Both come with flanges for stapling. The only real difference is length: blankets come 8 feet long, while batts are 4 feet long. There is also roll insulation of almost any length, for all practical purposes.

Batt and blanket insulation come with and without a vapor barrier, which is a foil or treated paper surface (on one side). This barrier helps to keep heat in the house. Buy it with the vapor barrier, and when installing the insulation make sure that the vapor barrier faces the warm side of the house (Fig. 213). For example, if on studs it would face the inside of the room, but on ceiling beams it would face down.

Insulation should be installed wherever warm and cold surfaces meet. In a room addition, then, it should be inserted between the wall studs and between the ceiling beam, or in some cases, the rafters.

INSTALLATION

To install a batt or blanket, first unroll it, then push it gently into the

Figure 213. Insulation's vapor barrier (shiny side) must always face warm side of room. If there are pipes, install the insulation behind them.

Figure 214. Most contractors will staple insulation flanges to studs as shown, but this can create problems of moisture getting behind insulation.

cavity between framing members, trying not to compress it. Insulation insulates because of the way it "stratifies" air, and pushing it down will militate against this ability.

Next, press the flange on the facing edge of the framing member and staple the insulating material tightly to it (Fig. 214). Place staples about 6 inches apart. When doing adjacent areas, staple the flanges over the ones already in place. Most professionally installed insulation is installed with flanges stapled to the insides of framing members, to make the Sheetrock a little easier to put on. But this approach is wrong because the open edge of the flanges allows the warm air to pass the insulation.

Fill all voids between framing members, including areas under windows (Fig. 215). If there are narrow spaces to fill, cut insulation (shears work well) in strips and stuff it in the cavities.

It is a good idea, when installing insulation, to wear gloves and a mask. Also, if you tear the insulating material while putting it in place, patch it with duct tape. If the hole is left uncovered, the vapor barrier seal will be ineffective.

In most instances—assuming normal height members—you can install blankets. If roll insulation is needed for the length, the installation is still the same.

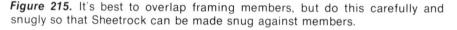

Figure 215. It's best to overlap framing members, but do this carefully and snugly so that Sheetrock can be made snug against members.

CHAPTER **15**

Sheetrocking

The standard wall material for rooms is Sheetrock, at least for the do-it-yourselfer. Learning to apply plaster is simply one of those skills that can be learned only by long experience.

Sheetrock is commonly available in 4 x 8 foot sheets and in ⅜-, ½-, and ⅝-inch thicknesses. It is also available in 6-, 7-, 10-, 12-, and 16-foot lengths. Usually, the ⅝-inch thickness is used only for fireproofing walls and is available in 4 x 8 sheets simply because it would be too heavy in larger sizes.

PLANNING

Before you start the job, plan it with the general criterion in mind that you will use the largest pieces available. Prepare to do the ceiling first. If the extension allows, use large pieces that will cover from wall to wall. The Sheetrock panels are tapered on the sides so they will accept a number of layers of sealing compound, yet still maintain a relatively flat surface.

Plan to install the walls horizontally, rather than vertically, a common mistake. Horizontal installation minimizes taping and makes joints easier to get at than if you have to go floor to ceiling. On ceilings, it is almost always better to run the panels at right angles to the joists. It will also be easier to tape if you stagger panel ends on joists. This will mean a number of short joints to tape rather than a few long ones. Since ends aren't tapered (only sides), this can be problematic.

CUTTING SHEETROCK

The best tool to use for cutting Sheetrock is a utility knife. Lean the panel against a wall, set a metal straightedge on it, then score through the paper on the front side. (A 4-foot T square may also be used as a cutting guide.) Then, bend the panel on the cut to break the plaster and use the utility knife to cut through the paper from the backside. When cutting, make the cut line ¼ inch shorter than your measurements indicate. The cutting method produces rough edges and this shorter dimension will enable these edges to mesh better when the pieces are butted.

BEGINNING WITH THE CEILING

Start on the ceiling. Use sawhorses and a stout piece of plywood laid across them so that your head and your helper's (required) will be about 3 inches from the ceiling.

Before installing ceiling panels, mark the locations of the joists on the plate. As you nail the panels up, you can refer to these marks to know where the joists are.

Lift the first panel up and jam it into a corner. Use a few Sheetrock nails to secure it along the side edges. (Do this quickly—the panel will want to pull through the nails.)

Then secure the panel to the joists. Do the ends last.

Each nail should be driven slightly beneath the surface, dimpling the paper (Fig. 216). Place all nails 7 to 8 inches apart. If you break the paper covering, it can be patched with joint tape.

Butt the next panel adjacent to the first with the tapered sides together. If you wish, you can make the panel easier to support by securing pieces of wood to the joists (Fig. 217). These form lip ledges that hold the Sheetrock by the edges.

Most ceilings are likely to be out of square—up to 2 inches is not uncommon. So before you install panels that abut the wall, measure from the last installed ceiling panel to the wall in a number of different places so you can trim the last panel at the proper angle.

ELECTRICAL BOX

It is likely that you will want an electrical fixture in the center of the ceiling. Before covering it with Sheetrock, mark where it is to be located. To do this, use a square, marking where the sides of the box fall on the last installed panel, and its distance from the edge. Then, when you cover the box with a panel you'll know where the box is hidden. You can remove Sheetrock over the box with a keyhole saw, using a utility knife to clean up the edges of the opening.

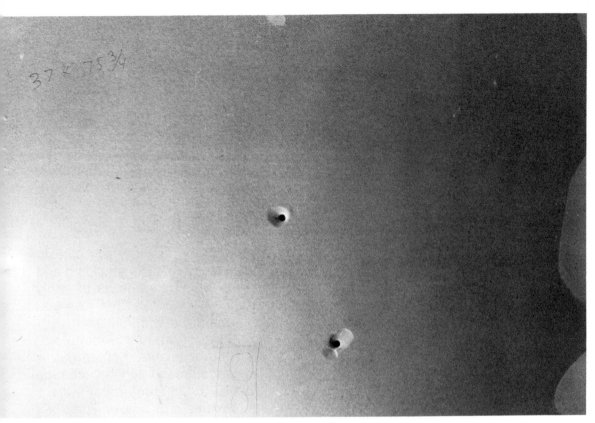

Figure 216. All nails should be set in surface so that paper dimples.

Figure 217. Nailing a piece of molding loosely to the ceiling member is a good way to support Sheetrock panels on the ceiling while you nail them.

WALLS

As mentioned, it's best to install Sheetrock panels horizontally. Before installing any panels, mark off stud locations on the ceiling panels and on the floor. As you install the panels, you'll know where the studs are.

Assuming a standard 8-foot-high ceiling, install the first panel in a corner, jockeying it up into place and nailing it to plate and studs. Then install the one under it, also nailing it to studs with nails 7 to 8 inches apart. If the ceiling is a few inches higher than 8 feet, install the first panel as mentioned, then install the one below it so its bottom edge rests against the floor. This will leave a narrow gap between panels, which can be filled with a strip of Sheetrock. Or, you could eliminate the gap by butting the panels and using a high baseboard to cover the gap at the floor line.

Proceed as above around the room. It's a good idea to butt panels against a door or window or above them (Fig. 218). This will cut down the amount of taping you will have to do as you'll have a short joint instead of a long one. Only one of the corner panels needs to be nailed. The edge of one will hold the other in place. If you find that any wall area is shorter than 4 feet, install a piece of panel vertically. This will cut down or eliminate the necessity of taping.

When all of the paneling has been installed, install the outside metal corner beading; this material is purchased when you buy the paneling, and it protects corners from chipping. Press it in place gently and snugly and nail it securely.

SPACKLING AND TAPING

If you take your time, you can do quite a presentable job spackling and taping. The key, though, is to apply the material smoothly: the less you have to sand the better.

A number of tapes and joint compounds are available. For an easier job, we recommend 2-inch-wide tape (it comes in 250-foot rolls) with a rough texture and tiny perforations (stay away from large-holed paper). Of the joint compounds, the common premixed kind (not the vinyl) is recommended. It comes at the proper consistency and is easy to work with and apply.

In terms of tools, you'll need a hawk for holding small amounts of the compound, a 4- to 5-inch flexible broad knife, and a 5 x 11 steel trowel. For corners, you can obtain a specialized corner knife, but this is not absolutely essential.

What to Tape

You have a choice as to whether you want to use tape between wall and ceiling panels. You can use crown or cove (easier) molding as an alternative. But molding can shrink, causing a gap to occur

Figure 218. Last piece of Sheetrock panel to be installed is butted above opening.

between panels, whereas tape will not gap. Corners are also taped, as well as wherever panels butt together.

It's a good idea to tape the flat areas first to gain some facility with the broad knife. The technique is to scoop a good size ball of compound about the size of a grapefruit onto the hawk. With the broad knife, apply the compound about ⅛ inch thick and 6 inches wide to the full length of the joint, spreading it on very evenly (Fig. 219). Check to make sure the compound is smooth and free of lumps. Cut a piece of joint tape as long as the joint, center it on the joint, and press it into place with your fingers. Use the knife again to embed the tape, working from the middle toward the ends, and pressing hard so the tape is stretched (Fig. 220).

Use this technique on all joints. On corner joints, apply a 3-inch-wide strip of compound down both edges of the corner. Here, the best technique is to set a ball of the material on the knife, hold the working edge vertically at the ceiling, and run the knife down the wall. The corner should be "filled" completely with joint compound.

Next, cut and fold the tape in half lengthwise and press it into the corner with your fingers, then smooth each edge of the corner separately with the broad knife. If you use a corner knife—which is shaped to fit the corner—you can do both edges at the same time. Here, there will be a slight excess of compound

beyond the edge of the knife that should be removed with the broad knife. Check as you apply tape that it is adhering well. If it isn't, it means that not enough compound is being used.

The first coat must be allowed to dry completely before the second coat, and between it and the finish coat.

Apply the second coat 3 inches wider on both sides than the first (Fig. 221). Concentrate on filling in tapered edges of the first coat. Apply the final coat 3 inches (on both sides) beyond the second coat. Throughout, concentrate on blending in each coat so there are no raised edges and no lumps. Press a little harder with each succeeding coat, remove particles of materials, and fill all holes. When finished, all the coats should be not more than ¹/₁₆ inch thick, and should be about 18 inches wide.

Dimpled nailheads should also be covered with compound, as well as outside corner beading. There is no rule on how many coats to use. Just use enough so that the areas are smooth—two is normal for nailheads while corner beads will take at least three to make smooth.

The time it takes compound to dry will vary between two and forty-eight hours.

As mentioned earlier, a good smooth spackling job will keep you from much sanding. After spackling, though, you should sand, using No. 80 paper, to remove any slight irregularities.

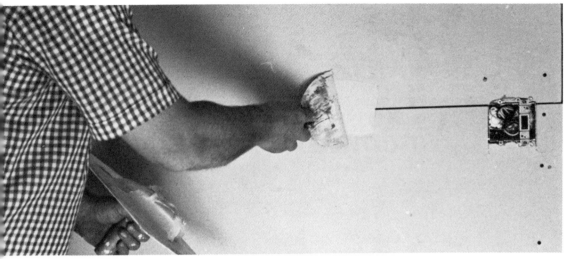

Figure 219. Apply joint compound over all joints.

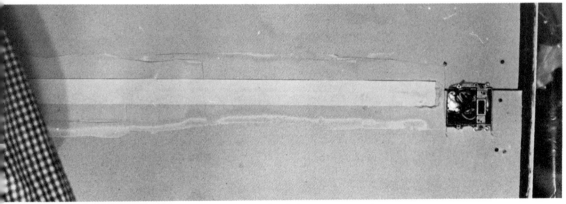

Figure 220. Use knife to apply tape over the joint compound.

Figure 221. Apply a second thin coat of compound and let dry, then apply additional coats.

CHAPTER **16**

Window and Door Molding

All windows and doors are trimmed with molding. On a standard double-hung window, start the job by installing the stool, the interior ledge that is often mistakenly called the sill. It comes in various thicknesses. It should extend ¾ inch beyond the casing, whatever width this will be. So, for example, if the casing were 2¼ inches wide, the molding should be long enough to extend 3 inches to either side of the window jamb.

Saw the stool to this length, then hold it against the bottom of the window, noting the sections, such as jambs and mullion, that will be recessed into it (Fig. 222). Use dividers or a ruler to mark the stool for these recesses, then cut out the sections with a fine-tooth handsaw and coping saw (Fig. 223). You can leave the ends square or round them off with a small block plane. When notched out, nail the stool in place.

WINDOW-STOP MOLDING

Stop moldings are the narrow strips that provide the finishing touches. They go on next. Three pieces are required—two for the sides and one across the top. Usually, the stop width will be the same as the distance from the face of the bottom sash to the inside edge of the jamb; to be sure, though, measure it.

First, cut all pieces to approximate

Figure 222. Stool on window must be notched out to fit over jambs and mullion.

Figure 223. Notched-out stool would look like this. Dividers are handy in taking measurements.

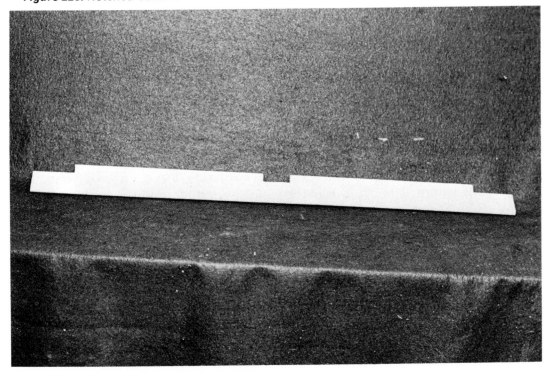

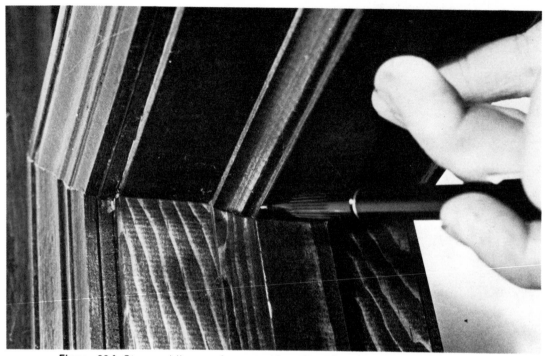

Figure 224. Stop molding on door must be mitered and coped to fit at corners.

length, making sure one end is square. Hold the top piece in place with the square end of the jamb and the other overlapping the other side. Mark it there, then cut the piece to length and secure with 3d finishing nails.

Hold one of the side pieces with the square end resting on the stool and mark where it crosses the top jamb. Repeat the procedure on the other side. Cut miter joints and cope the pieces to fit against the head stop; nail in place (Fig. 224). Finally, countersink nails and fill the holes.

The window stop may form part of the track that the sash rides in. Therefore, it's important to nail it so that the window won't bind. Try the window both before and after the nails are countersunk. If it binds, use a chisel to pry it away so the sash rides freely.

THE DOOR STOP

To install the door stop, use the measuring techniques as for the window stop. Install the headpiece first with the door closed and latched. Secure the stop so it has $1/16$-inch clearance between itself and the door. Before you install additional pieces, try the door to make sure it doesn't bind.

With the head stop in place, cut and secure the sidepieces. Nail the hinge sidepiece on first, then try the door. If okay, install the other sidepiece. If any piece binds, you can move it by tapping with a block of wood and a hammer.

CASING

Door casing has two sides and one headpiece miter-jointed together. When casing is installed around the door, about ⅛ inch of the jamb edge remains exposed. Start by standing the hinge sidepiece in place and mark a 45-degree angle on it from the corner of the door frame. Cut the piece at a 45-degree angle (one-half of the miter joint) and tack it in place. Set the headpiece in place, and mark and cut a corresponding miter and tack this piece in place. Trim the joint as needed to make sure the miter fits well. (A block plane can be useful here.)

Next, put the headpiece in place and mark the wall at a 45-degree angle extending from the corner of the frame. Stand the sidepiece in place and mark where it intersects the line. Replace the headpiece and transfer the marks to it, then do the same with the sidepiece. Cut the miter and tack the pieces in place, carefully fitting them together; finally, nail everything up solid. Use 3d finishing nails in the thin side of the molding and 6d nails through the wide side and into the studs. If you cut the pieces a little off, you can always raise the sidepieces to close the miter.

Window Casing

Follow the procedure described above for installing the door casing, except that the edge of the jamb should be completely covered. There should also be an apron under the stool. You can use a piece of casing cut square at the ends for this.

All nails on casing should be countersunk and the holes filled with putty when the job is finished.

Window- and Door-Casing Types

There are various kinds of casings available for doors and windows. One popular type is clamshell, which is 2¼ inches wide, thin on one side and thick (⅝ inch) on the other. Another type is Colonial, which may be 2¼ or 2½ inches. Here, the face is molded in a design, unlike clamshell casing, which is plain-faced. In any case, installation procedure is the same.

If only a few pieces are required, you can cut miter joints by using a sharp handsaw and a 45-degree L square. For extensive cutting, however, get a miter box—it will make the job much easier. Many kinds are available, but you should obtain the best you can afford. You definitely won't regret it.

INDEX